Law Enforcement and Cross Border Terrorism

About the Author

Sankar Sen, former Director General, National Human Rights Commission, New Delhi and former Director of the National Police Academy, Hyderabad, joined the Indian Police Service in 1960. He graduated from Presidency College, Calcutta and obtained Master's degree in History from Calcutta University. He was allotted to Orissa cadre and held a number of posts with distinction. He joined the Border Security Force as the Inspector General in 1987 and was later on promoted as the Additional Director General. Thereafter, he was posted as the Director of the SVP National Police Academy (NPA), the premier institution for training of the senior police officers in the country.

He was awarded the Police Medal for meritorious service in 1979 and President's Police Medal for distinguished service in 1986. On completion of his assignment in the NPA, he joined as the Director General of the National Human Rights Commission and later on functioned as the Special Rapporteur, in charge of custodial justice programmes of the NHRC. He has to his credit many books including *Police Today and Human Rights in a Developing Society;* and *Tryst with Law Enforcement and Human Rights.* At present he is a Senior Fellow in the Institute of Social Sciences, New Delhi.

LAW ENFORCEMENT AND CROSS BORDER TERRORISM

SANKAR SEN
IPS (Retd.)

CONCEPT PUBLISHING COMPANY, NEW DELHI-110059

Cataloging in Publication Data—DK

Courtesy: D.K. Agencies (P) Ltd. <docinfo@dkagencies.com>

Sen, Sankar, 1936-
Law enforcement and cross border terrorism/ Sankar Sen.
p. cm.
Includes bibliographical references.
Includes index.
ISBN 8180691683

1. Law enforcement—India. 2. Insurgency—India.
3. Terrorism. I. Title.

DDC 355.133 230 954 21

ISBN-81-8069-168-3

First Published 2005

Published and Printed by
Ashok Kumar Mittal
Concept Publishing Company,
A/15-16, Commercial Block, Mohan Garden,
New Delhi-110059 (INDIA)

Phones : 25351460, 25351794
Fax : 091-11-25357103
Email : publishing@conceptpub.com

Preface

The book contains a bunch of articles covering different issues of law enforcement and complex security problems thrown up by cross border terrorism afflicting the country. They appeared in different national dailies in the course of last three years. Policing a pluralistic democratic society is always a difficult and challenging job, and the police are often at the receiving ends of criticism, both fair and unfair. Police constitute the most visible symbol of the authority of the state. Efficient and humane law enforcement by the police strengthens the legitimacy of the government by demonstrating that the authority of the state can be used effectively in favour of the people. Indeed, responsible and service-oriented policing will do more for the legitimacy of the government than any other social programme with immediate and visible effect.

Unfortunately, for a variety of factors, historical as well as political, police in India often serve the partisan ends of the regime in power and do not function as upholders of the rights of the people. This alienates the police from the public. In democracy, police must be governed by the rule of law and not guided by directions given arbitrarily by regimes in power.

For achieving this objective, there is need for structural reforms in Indian police as well as commitment on the part of the police and political leadership to effect organizational changes. If there is lack of interest and commitment of the senior leadership, police reforms cannot be brought about by stealth from below. Democratic police reforms will not be possible by infusion of more resources, but by changing the management priorities and culture of the organisation and realization on the part of the police rank and file that changes will help them to discharge their work better.

Reforms must incorporate their own insights and on-the-job knowledge. There is also need for public understanding of the constraints and the problems of the police.

Some of the other articles touch upon the different patterns and problems of cross-border terrorism. For nearly two decades cross border terrorism is posing serious threats to national security and integrity. It has taken a tragic toll of the lives of more than 29000 civilians and 5000 security personnel and imposed a mind-boggling sum of Rs. 64000 crores in security-related operations. Despite new peace initiatives with Pakistan, the chances of immediate resolution of the problem are not very encouraging. Adversarial relationship with Pakistan is not going to end soon and progress in this direction is going to be slow. We have to remain on our guard and keep the powder dry. However, the most effective answer to terrorism is not just the preparedness of the security forces and intelligence outfits, but the support and cooperation of the alert and well-informed citizenry. It is necessary to educate the public of the goals and the tactics of the terrorists and ensure their support for counter-terrorist operations of the government.

It is a fact that because of escalating terrorist violence and attendant public disorder, the democratization of the police receives a setback. The police tend to develop a fortress mentality and start functioning like the army. There is greater emphasis on building police resources and capacity than on reforms. There is intermingling of police and military functions to the detriment of humane and democratic policing.

I hope the articles will elicit interest of the law enforcement officers, academics, informed members of the public on issues and complexities concerning policing and a myriad of problems thrown up by cross border terrorism and strategies to be fashioned to deal with them.

I am grateful to Mr. C. R. Irani, Editor, Statesman, for giving kind permission to use the articles earlier published in the Statesman.

Sankar Sen

Contents

SECTION I

Law Enforcement

1

Massacre at Boraibari

Ghastly killing of 16 Border Security Force (BSF) personnel has caused a sense of anger and horror all over the country and cast a shadow on the friendly relations between India and Bangladesh. Former Director General of BSF, Prakash Singh, in a statement released to the press raised a number of pertinent questions. He held the government responsible for mishandling the issue and expressed the view that the ill-fated BSF foray into Boraibari in Bangladesh must have had some kind of clearance from Delhi. He was correct in pointing out that the pictures of mutilated bodies of BSF personnel will have a very demoralising effect on the minds of BSF jawans guarding the borders of the country.

Regarding this gory incident, I have somewhat different views and perceptions. I have had the privilege of serving the BSF first as the Inspector General in West Bengal Frontier and thereafter as the Additional Director General for nearly five years. I had visited the nook and corner of the long and porous Indo-Bangladesh border, and particularly the border between West Bengal and Bangladesh. I feel that only a thorough inquiry will reveal the chain of tragic events and circumstances culminating in the massacre of the BSF jawans at Boraibari. However for understanding and appreciating this grim and unsavoury development some important facts have to be borne in mind.

First, the long 4,096 km border between India and Bangladesh does not follow everywhere natural geographical alignments. It moves in a crisscross manner through the densely populated villages, long green paddy fields, innumerable perennial and seasonal rivers and nalas. At the time of country's partition the boundary line drawn on the map by the Boundary Commission under Radcliff was straightaway implemented on the ground due to the paucity of time at the Commission's disposal. The entire border, and more so between West Bengal and Bangladesh, is thickly populated. There is a large concentration of population in villages on either side of the border. A number of villages extend up to zero line on the border and strangely enough there are bordering villages with parts of them in India and parts in Bangladesh. Indeed one gets a feeling that the partition of the country made historically possible what is geographically impossible.

Second, there are 111 Indian enclaves in Bangladesh and 51 Bangladesh enclaves inside India. The 6.5 km stretch of the border is yet to be demarcated. The demarcation of the unmarked 6.5 km of the border is pending because of the concern of the Hindu population living on the lands which are likely to go to Bangladesh after demarcation. Lands have to be found to resettle these people before the demarcation becomes finally operative. Bangladesh ratified the Indira-Mujib Boundary Agreement in November 1974. But it has not so far been ratified by India, because the parliamentary approval has not been so far obtained. This is unfortunate and creates a feeling in the minds of the Bangladeshis that India is not serious about it.

Third, the recent tension and skirmishes in the Indo-Bangladesh border are related to the issue of adverse possession. Pyrdiwah is a small Khasi village of about 20 families near Dawky at Assam-Bangladesh border. It is located on a plot of land about 300 acres inside Bangladesh and the BSF border outpost (BOP) is also located on this plot in adverse possession of India. On April 15, 2001 about 1000 Bangladesh Rifles (BDR) men surrounded the post from three sides. They also chased away the local villagers. BSF

Force, however, held its ground. Incidents of this kind are not new. Similar incidents had also occurred in the past. The BSF would bring in reinforcements, exchange fire with BDR, and then have a flag meeting. On numerous occasions there were clashes between the villagers on two sides of the long border leading to confrontation between the BSF and BDR.

I still recollect an incident in Murshidabad district in West Bengal where following clashes between the villagers on two sides of the border, there was heavy exchange of fire between BSF and BDR. DIG Bangladesh Rifles immediately got in touch with me over phone and skirmishes came to an end and tension subsided after the flag meeting. Both BSF and BDR are equipped with automatic rifles and mortars. In this exchange of fire three or four BDR constables and one BSF jawan died. When I visited the spot, the local villagers gave me a hero's welcome and I was overwhelmed with emotion to find that they had installed a statue of the BSF jawan, who had laid down his life for protecting their hearths and homes. There were many occasions when BDR complained of somewhat aggressive tactics by BSF and in some cases I found that there was some substance in their allegations. After some time tension would subside and *status quo* would return. Sometimes during flag meetings and border co-operation conferences with BDR, some of the BSF Commandants used to behave uppishly, if not rudely, and on one occasion I had to pull up a senior BSF officer for unnecessarily throwing about his weight. There was display of Big brother attitude and lack of appreciation of the sensitivities of a small neighbour. Some of the BDR officers had personally unburdened their feelings to me in this regard.

However, BSF foray into Boraibari was a grave operational blunder resulting in this tragic loss of lives. Boraibari is in Kurigram District of Bangladesh bordering Assam, a plot of land in adverse possession of an Indian enclave inside Bangladesh. It is not exactly known what prompted the BSF personnel to move into Boraibari. Only a thorough inquiry will unravel the truth behind this misadventure. Articles and news items have been published in various journals and newspapers suggesting that the BSF operation was taken after obtaining clearance from Delhi. Prakash Singh has also expressed the view that this ill-fated operation had some kind of clearance from Delhi. I, however, have a feeling that after Pyrdiwah incident, BSF decided to aggressively patrol the border and cock a snook at the BDR. The decision for intrusion into Boraibari perhaps was taken at a local level, at the level of Frontier IG or at the local BSF Commandant. General order for border alert was issued by BSF headquarters, but this counter-strike was perhaps the brain-child of the local Commandant. I feel this because I have seen examples of thoughtless aggressive action by the BSF in the past. The truth would come to light after the enquiry, which has been ordered. I also cannot fathom as to why the BSF jawans were mercilessly killed and their bodies mutilated. In the past, whenever BSF jawans intruding inside Bangladesh have been captured by the BDR, they have all been returned after a flag meeting without any harm being done to them. BSF also did the same thing in respect of BDR personnel. I feel that the local BSF Commandant, Mondal, when surrounded by the villagers did not open fire to avoid blood bath, but this lynching was done by the local villagers who had scores to settle with the BSF. But what baffles me is that why did not BDR contingent, instead of preventing, allowed this ghastly torture and killing. Only a thorough enquiry will uncover the whole truth.

It is reported in the press that present D.G., BSF, Gurubachan Jagat, has said that three patrol parties entered Boraibari, and one group led by the Deputy Commandant, Mondal, was captured by the BDR. However if BSF jawans were shot dead in captivity by the BDR personnel, it would be a wanton and shocking act of brutality.

Tension and anger among the BSF personnel is

understandable, but it is a wise decision not to allow them in the name of redeeming national honour to go for counter-strikes with a view to teaching a lesson to their counterparts in Bangladesh. This kind of retaliatory action would be short-sighted. Though BSF senior officers as well as jawans feel frustrated and seethe with anger, but this is the time to remain calm, exercise restraint and take measures after careful consideration.

Tension in Indo-Bangladesh border is closely linked with infiltration from Bangladesh. Political instability, inadequate economic development, and population explosions are some of the causative factors compelling a large number of *Bangladeshis* to leave their homes and enter India in search of employment. Many of them have settled down in the border districts of West Bengal and Assam and created an explosive problem. Somehow, state governments, particularly West Bengal and Assam, have not been alive to the gravity and magnitude of the problem. In meetings and conferences, the officers of BDR have consistently taken the stand that there had been no infiltration from Bangladesh and refused to take back the *Bangladeshis* handed over to them by us. We suggested to the state government of West Bengal to introduce identity cards initially in some of the border areas in West Bengal where infiltration have become an alarming menace. But the state government had dragged its feet.

Meanwhile, the wider issues of settling the territorial disputes with Bangladesh pending since 1947 viz. enclaves in each other's, issues of adverse possession and clear demarcation of 6.5 km unmarked border should be speeded up. There can no longer be any pussy-footing over them. Further, BSF strength in the eastern border has to be augmented. At present, it is thinly spread and gaps between the Border Outposts (Bops) in this populous and porous border are too wide. However, this incident which must have caused deep misunderstanding between the top brass of

BDR and BSF should not trigger off further clashes between these two forces and turn the peaceful border into a combustible one.

—27 May, 2001, The Statesman

2

Hostile Witnesses

Instances of key witnesses turning hostile and irretrievably spoiling the cases for prosecution are not rare. However, recent reports of witnesses turning hostile and blatantly resiling from their earlier statements before the police in some sensational cases (like that of Jessica Lall) have shocked the conscience of the civil society and shattered its faith in the working of the criminal justice system. Witnesses are being bullied or gained over by the lure of lucre and they without any moral compunction retract from their statements made earlier before the police. The upshot is the acquittal of persons responsible for commission of heinous crimes—triumph of the devils and sorrow for angels. "When a criminal goes free" says Lord Devlin, "it is as much a failure of the abstract justice as when an innocent man is convicted".

In 1998, the All India Conviction rate, i.e. ratio of the cases convicted to the total cases tried in courts was 37.4 per cent which was marginally lower than 38.2 per cent in 1997 (*Crimes in India*, 1998, published by the National Crime Records Bureau). But conviction rate in heinous offences was less than 10 per cent. The mounting acquittal figures only go to embolden the criminals, who now know that the gains of crime far outweigh the risks of crime.

Recently, the Supreme Court was constrained to observe in a case (State of Bengal *vs*. Mir Muhammad Omar and others) that the job of the trial court is not to be wasted by picking out lapses in investigation and expressing unsavoury criticisms against the investigating officers.

"Courts should bear in mind the time constraint of the police officers in the present system, ill-equipped machinery they have to cope with and the traditional apathy of respectable persons to come forward for giving evidence in the criminal cases. These are the realities the police forces have to confront with while conducting investigation in almost every case."

Reluctance of the members of the public to depose in criminal cases is due mainly to distrust of the police and inordinate delay in the disposal of cases in courts of law. The Supreme Court while delivering its Constitutional Bench Judgement in the case of Abdul Rehman Antulay *vs.* R. S. Nayak declared that right to speedy trial is implicit in Article 21 of the Constitution and thus constitutes a fundamental right of every person accused of a crime. Further, public interest also demands that criminal justice should be swift and guilty should be punished while the events are fresh in public mind, and "further it is undesirable to let things settle till memories have grown dim to truth". Pronouncements of the apex court, however, have not improved the situation on the ground. Delay ordinarily prejudices the prosecution. Public interest in the cases diminishes. Witnesses become non-available and the accused persons, particularly the rich and the powerful, utilise all possible and available means to win over the witnesses.

There are various reasons for the reluctance of the witnesses to come forward and depose correctly and in a straightforward manner. First, the manner of conducting investigation by the police is very often rude, overbearing and also inconsiderate. Second, as cases drag on in courts with frequent adjournments very little regard is paid for the convenience of the witnesses. The allowances paid to them are meagre. Even the pocket expenses incurred by them are not reimbursed by anybody. Loss of wages for a number of days cause substantial suffering to many poor witnesses. And that is why a feeling prevails, particularly among common people, that to get embroiled as a witness is like being played as a fish on a long line. Third, witnesses fear retaliation, particularly when the accused persons are influential people. Woe betide the innocent persons who venture to speak. They may incur the wrath of hardened criminals and lose their lives or limbs. Maharashtra Police Commission 1962 in its recommendations made a special point of the need to give protection to the people who testify against the goondas. There is similar need to provide protection to the witnesses who come forward to depose against the terrorists. Fourth, there is a prevalence of the belief in public mind in Indian society that the individual has no duty to assist the police in criminal matters, and prevention and investigation of crime is the sole responsibility of the police. This kind of myopia also prevails in other countries, but it is more acute in India because as a perceptive foreign observer, David Bayley (Police and Political Development in India—page 163), puts it, "its citizen are submerged in their small family and community circles and their foremost duties are confined within these circles". Fifth there is also general human reluctance to get involved in unpleasant situation, particularly in regard to serious crimes that involve passions and personalities. This tendency of not getting entangled is now called 'Kitty Genovese Syndrome'—Kitty Genovese being the name of the girl in New York whose repeated cries for help when being violated by the hoodlums went unheeded because those who heard it remained passive onlookers and did not want to get involved.

Further now, sanctity of oaths in the courts has disappeared and the witnesses make false statements on oaths in the courts without any compunction. There is a telling folk-saying in Northern India "Speak the truth. You are not speaking in a court of law". Unfortunately, there are no hard data on the incidence and extent of perjury. Prosecutions are few and far between and hence available data do not reveal a clear picture.

Provision of the criminal law based on distrust of the police also encourages this foul game by the witnesses and affects the fate of the cases. Section 160 of the Criminal Procedure Code Empowers a police officer making an investigation to examine "persons who appear to be acquainted with the circumstances of the cases". Section 161 (2) lays down that "Such persons shall be bound to answer all questions relating to such case put to him by said officer, other than questions the answer to which would have a tendency to expose him to a criminal charge or to a penalty of forfeiture". In the old Criminal Procedure Code of 1882, the sub-section was worded somewhat differently. The person was then required to answer all questions "truly" put to him by a police officer. The word 'truly' has been omitted from the new Cr.P.C. now in force. Delhi Police Commission strongly recommended (Report of the Delhi Police Commission, page 175) that sub-section (2) of Section 161 Cr. P.C. should be amended and the 'truly' inserted after such 'person shall be bound to answer'. A witness called by the police should be under a legal obligation to disclose truly the facts within his knowledge.

The National Police Commission in its report (Fourth Report of the National Police Commission, Chapter XXVII, page 5) recommended that the statement of a witness recorded by a Police Officer need not be signed by the witness, but a copy of the such statement duly authenticated by the Police Officer recording it shall be handed over to the witness whose statement was recorded, if so desired by that person. In the eyes of law this position would be slightly different from obtaining his signature on the very statement itself, but would be a sufficient safeguard to ensure that the record as made by the Police Officer is not a deviation from what the witness had told him. The Law Commission of India (154th Report) endorsed similar amendment.

Again Section 162 of the Cr.P.C., provides that a statement recorded by the police in the course of investigation shall not be signed by the person making the statements. This ban on a witness signing his own statement stems from the same distrust of the police that makes confession before the police inadmissible in evidence (Section 25 of the Indian Evidence Act). This frequently enables the witnesses to resile from the statements made by them before the police in the courts of law. In England, statements before the police are generally signed by the witnesses and considerable importance is attached to them, because it is difficult to confute such statements.

Law Commission in its 14th Report (Volume II, page 753) suggested that the statement of a witness should be reduced to writing and signed by him, provided the witness is capable of reading what has been recorded. The Commission observed that 'psychologically, persons who have witnessed the commission of an offence are eager to state the true version if they are questioned soon after the commission of the offence and before the memory of the events had faded and before other considerations or influence have worked on them'. In the light of the behaviour of the witnesses in many cases where influential persons are involved, Section 162 of the Cr.P.C. should be so amended that a police officer may obtain the signature of a literate witness on the record of his statement made during the investigation of a case.

The Punjab Police Commission (1961-62) also opined that Section 162 of the Cr.P.C. should be amended as recommended by the Law Commission. The Punjab Police Commission felt that it is necessary to make this amendment in view of the fact that in a large number of cases, witnesses resile from the statements made to the police as a result of the persuasion of the defence and as a result of the sympathy the people feel towards the accused after his arrest. Public opinion is generally sympathetic towards a person who is subjected to crime like—rape, murder, and dacoity but as time elapses, sympathy changes towards the accused and his friends and relatives, and as the statements under Sections

161 and 162 are not signed by the witnesses they can resile from them.

On the recommendations of the Law Commission in its Forty-first Report (September, 1969), a provision was introduced in the Code of Criminal Procedure Bill, 1970, to authorise the Police Officer to obtain the signature of a witness on the statement recorded from him in cases where the witness can read the statement so recorded. But the Joint Committee of Parliament felt that this provision may lead to abuse, and therefore, rejected it.

To check the increasing trend of witnesses turning hostile, the Law Commission has now proposed that Section 164 should be made mandatory for the investigating officers. They should get statements of all material witnesses questioned during investigation recorded on oath before the magistrate. This would prevent witnesses from turning hostile at their free will. No doubt, this will be a check, but to get all the material witnesses mandatorily examined before a magistrate under Section 164 of Cr.P.C. in all cases will be time-taking and will further slow down the investigation.

—28 July, 2001, The Statesman

3

To Fight Terror, POTO is Necessary

The Prevention of Terrorism Ordinance (POTO) has sparked off animated, and at times, angry discussions and debates. It will also dominate proceeding in the winter session of the Parliament. Many political parties, lawyers and human rights activists are up in arms against the Ordinance. They have dubbed it as a black law and expressed misgivings that this is likely to be misused like the previous. Terrorist and Disruptive Activities (Prevention) Act (TADA). Past abuses will be re-visited. The Chairman, National Human Rights Commission, has also gone on record that the Ordinance is unnecessary and the existing laws, if properly enforced and implemented, are adequate to combat the menace of terrorism. Leaders of the government and many senior law-enforcement officers, however, decry this 'Poto phobia' and favour a powerful and effective law to arm the law enforcement agencies to take on the terrorists. Thus the battle-lines are sharply drawn.

It may be recalled that the Terrorist and Disruptive Activities (Prevention) Act (TADA) lapsed in May 1995. The constitutionality of the Act was upheld by the Supreme Court in the case of Kartar Singh *vs.* State of Punjab (1994). Again, in the Sanjay Dutt's case also (Sanjay Dutt *vs.* State, 1994) the Supreme Court speaking through Justice Shri J.S. Verma justified the existence of TADA by observing that it was enacted to cope with the 'escalating terrorist violence in the country', and there were materials before the court to indicate that the foreign agencies were active in assisting the flow of arms into the country and the felt-need of the time was to strike a balance between the interests of the nation and the rights of the TADA accused. Further, the court held the view that the mere possibility of misuse did not affect the constitutionality of the law.

However, gross misuse gave a foul odour to TADA. I was serving in the NHRC as the Director General (Investigation) when the Commission started reviewing the TADA cases along with the senior officers of the state governments. It was found that in many cases people had been detained under TADA with the oblique motive of depriving the accused persons from getting bails. As a result of reviewing, the number of TADA cases drastically came down from 60,000 to 6,700. The state government that misused it most was Gujarat under Chimanbhai Patel. Even though the state was not plagued by terrorism, the Gujarat Government had jailed about 19,000 persons under TADA. It was flagrantly misused against the workers of the Bharatiya Kisan Union and many bootleggers and ordinary criminals. The Bihar Government had not even given official notification of the implementation of TADA, but some of the Superintendents of Police on their own initiative, as the then Home Commissioner of Bihar told the NHRC, implemented the act in their own districts.

Though TADA was not renewed because of widespread criticisms, there was clear and definite feeling in many knowledgeable quarters that the country needed a strong and special law to combat the hydra-headed monster called terrorism. I recall that the officials of the Home Department of the Government of United Kingdom, who visited the NHRC in 1995 during discussions with us clearly expressed the view that the police and the security forces would not be able to checkmate the terrorists without a stringent anti-terrorist law.

It may be mentioned in this connection that the United Kingdom had enacted a major piece of anti-terrorist legislation—Prevention of Terrorism (Temporary Provisions)

Acts of 1974 and 1976. Following two bomb explosions in Birmingham Pubs on 2nd November 1974, in which 20 people died and 180 were injured, the British public opinion was convinced that emergency measures were needed to contain unabated terrorist violence. The Bill was subjected to only two hours debate in the House of Commons and approved without a division. The Bill gave power to the Home Secretary to proscribe an organization as illegal and authorized the police to detain suspects arrested under the Act for 48 hours and for a further five days with the Home Secretary's approval. The act of 1976 was re-enacted with amendments in the form of Prevention of Terrorism (Temporary Provisions) Act 1984 which gave power to the authorities to exclude persons from entry to the country in order to prevent terrorism and other extensive powers to deal with the terrorists. The British Police were not thus asked to deal with the menace of terrorism by the ordinary laws of the land, but at the same time were not allowed to misuse the law. Report of Lord Shackleton reviewing the operations of the Act recommended its continuance.

In this context, it may be borne in mind that the POTO is certainly not the outcome of a sudden brainwave of the Union Government. The Law Commission in the report released in April 2000, felt the need for a special law to deal with the terrorists, especially when terrorist operations have become complex, transnational and assumed form of a proxy war by a hostile neighbour. The Law Commission's report pointed out that cross-border terrorism till April 2001, had taken a toll of 30,000 civilians and 5,101 security personnel and cost the exchequer around Rs. 64,000 crores.

The special anti-terrorism ordinance (POTO) promulgated by the government is based on the Law Commission's recommendations and it excludes some of the obnoxious provisions of the TADA, which led to human rights violations. It includes some definite safeguards. First, Section 34 of the POTO provides for appeal against any judgement or order of the Special Courts to be set up to deal with offences under the Ordinance to the High Court both on facts and law. Earlier, TADA limited the possibility of appeal to one court, the Supreme Court and not to both the Supreme Court and the High Court as the Criminal Procedure Code provides. The Supreme Court in Kartar Singh's case observed that "the indisputable reality is that the Supreme Court is beyond the reach of the average person considering the fact of distance, expenditure, etc". Second, the period of police custody of a suspect has been reduced from 60 to 30 days and, as per section 51 of the Ordinance, the person arrested has to be informed of his right to consult a legal practitioner as soon as he is brought to the police station. The members of his family have to be informed of the arrest without delay and the arrestee shall be permitted to meet his legal representative during the course of interrogation. Third, section 59 of the Ordinance provides for constitution of Review Committees presided over by a person, who is or has been a judge of a High Court. The Review Committees are expected to provide safeguards against arbitrary and illegal detention. Fourth, the Ordinance contains provisions (Section 57) for punis hment of the police officers, exercising powers corruptly or maliciously and compensation to the victims of unlawful arrest or detention. The new Ordinance thus tries to take note of and provides safeguards against abuse and misuse that had earlier characterised the operation of TADA.

One of the main planks of criticism from many lawyers and human rights activists is that section 32 of the Ordinance makes certain confessions made to a police officer, not lower in rank than the Superintendent of Police, admissible in evidence. This is contrary to section 25 of the Indian Evidence Act 1872, which excludes from evidence confessions made before a police officer. It is necessary to stress from the angle of law-enforcement that this statutory distrust of the police is based not on any theory of jurisprudence or any logical formulation. It was incorporated in law in 1872, because the illiterate, untrained and lowly paid police officers of the time were not considered worthy of trust. Confessions before the police officers are admissible in evidence subject to prescribed safeguards in all advanced countries. However, no one wants that confessions before the police should be relied upon, if they are unfairly obtained. All that is wanted is that evidence obtained in such confessions must not be lost to the court which in any case is expected to rigorously scrutinise the evidence before coming to any conclusion. Further, it has to be borne in mind that regarding crimes committed by the terrorists, witnesses are unwilling to depose before the court due to the fear of retaliation by the terrorists, and there is hardly any existing arrangement to provide protection to the witnesses, who testify against the terrorists. It is a fact that but for the special rules of evidence under TADA which make confessions before the police admissible, not a single conviction would have been possible in the Rajiv Gandhi murder case. Further, the validity of a confession made by an arrested person under POTO will need to be endorsed before a magistrate before it can be considered as admissible in evidence in a court of law.

For granting of bail, the POTO lays down that no person accused of an offence punishable under the Ordinance shall be released on bail, unless the court gives the public prosecutor an opportunity of being heard. [Section 48 Clause (6)]. Senior law-enforcement officers can cite many cases, where release of dangerous criminals and terrorists on bail without justification helped them carry on further depredations to the detriment of the law-abiding ciltizens. At least, the court must hear the public prosecutor before deciding whether to release an accused terrorist on bail or not.

Again section 14 of the Ordinance prescribes obligations to furnish information regarding offence committed by the terrorists to the investigating officers and the failure to furnish information of deliberately giving false information is punishable. Similar provision exists in the U.K.'s Prevention of Terrorism (Temporary Provisions) Act 1984.

Law-enforcement authorities under the Ordinance are now empowered to seize immovable property provided they have reason to believe that it could be used for terrorism; while attaching such property relevant records and documents have to be produced before the Special Court within 48 hours.

Evidently, the hard fact has to be faced that after September 11, 2001 a new situation has emerged. Countries like the U.S. A., the U. K., Israel and India face risks of serious terrorist strikes. Induction of *Fidayeen* (suicide squads) has introduced a new dimension in Kashmir militancy. The fanatical terrorist groups unafraid of their own obliteration are likely to resort to devastating strikes against our vital assets not only in Kashmir, but also in different parts of the country and may use weapons of mass destruction—nuclear, biological and chemical. This kind of apocalypse is very much within the realm of possibility. Again Musharraf is likely to export to Kashmir many of the Talibans returning from Afghanistan, and this will significantly raise there the level of terror and violence. The existing criminal justice system is not designed to cope with a situation like this. To deal with this omnibus menace the police need powerful anti-terror laws to intercept communications, cutting off supply of funds, tracing the hideouts, seizing properties of the terrorists

In this context, it is worth mentioning that in the U.S.A., immediately after the Oklahama blast the omnibus, Anti Terrorism Bill (1995) was passed, which authorised summary trials, immediate deportation out of U.S. of persons suspected to constitute danger, and non-disclosure of the identity of the witnesses. Such provisions were thought necessary after two blasts in which 170 people had been killed. And now after September 11, the U.S. Congress introduced scores of Bills and legislations to fight terrorism. The U.S. Attorney General, John Ashcroft has also asked the Congress to upgrade and strengthen a number of laws to enhance anti-terrorist efforts. Similarly, stringent anti-terror laws have been passed by most of the European countries, who have not suffered even one thousandth of the casualties that have occurred in India, states like Karnataka and Maharashtra have preventive detention laws that have helped the police to tackle organised crime and terrorist operations.

Law-enforcement officers wedded to the cause of human right strongly feel that the "acts, methods and practices of terrorism in all its forms and manifestations, as emphasised in the declaration adopted in the World Conference in Vienna (1993) ... "are activities aimed at destruction of human rights". For effectively fighting against terrorism, states need stringent and anti-terrorist laws. The United Nations has also mandated that all states must adopt necessary legal instruments to prevent terrorism and strengthen international co-operation in combating terrorism. For successfully combating terrorism, the security forces have to be equipped with stringent and realistic anti-terrorist laws. It is necessary to arm them with powers, but at the same time, to ensure that they act within the four corners of law and do not misuse the authority. For this constant monitoring by the courts, review authorities and civil oversight agencies are called for.

—3 December, 2001, The Statesman

4

Gujarat Imbroglio—Can Gill Save the Day ?

Communal tension in Gujarat is continuing unabated. Armed clashes between rival communal groups are even now taking place and there is no knowing when communal peace and amity will be restored in that troubled state. Bomb blasts in Ahmedabad have now added another dimension to the problem. The decision of the state government, with pressures and proddings from the centre to appoint K.P.S. Gill as Police Adviser to the Chief Minister, Gujarat, is an unorthodox but welcome step. The success or otherwise of the experiment will depend on the political support, Gill will be able to get from the Chief Minister and his supporters in Gujarat. By any reckoning, Gill is an outstanding officer with charismatic leadership qualities. In the Punjab the revamped and re-energised the Punjab Police in their battle against terrorism and led them from the front. In my service career spanning over nearly four decades, I had interacted with him on many occasions and always appreciated his robust commonsense and pragmatic approach.

One of the key factors behind his success in the Punjab was the total support he received from Beant Singh, the then Chief Minister. Besides stiffening the spine and raising the morale of the Punjab Police, Gill was able to insulate it from external pulls and pressures. The rank and file looked upto him and not the political bosses for directions. There was no interference in the internal functioning of the Police.

Unfortunately, the Police in most of the states in India now have become totally politicised and subserve the partisan ends of their political masters. The police have become defenders of the establishment. And in utilising and manipulating the police for political ends, there is no difference among the ruling parties in different states. In a public opinion survey conducted by the Indian Institute of Public Opinion at the instance of the National Police Commission, it was found that majority of the respondents strongly felt that for the police, the political interference was a greater evil than corruption. In another recent survey conducted by the Second West Bengal Police Commission, the majority of the respondents clearly stated that "Policemen find it most difficult to take action against the criminals when they are politically connected".

Constant interference has also seriously disrupted the chain of command and control in the police. The Director General of Police has now very little say in the transfer and posting of the officers which is now being controlled by the Chief Minister or the Home Minister. Incidentally, the Chief Ministers hold charge of the Police Departments in almost all the states. This is a dramatic indication of the importance of the police in political life in contemporary India. A perceptive American author, David H. Bayley, has written that 'India which should have been expected to transform the organisation of the police rapidly after independence has exactly kept the same system which the British created after 1861. The control mechanism of the British Raj has survived and has been invigorated by a new dispersation'.

The National Police Commission nearly two decades ago in its reports dealing with various aspects of the police work and administration made salutary recommendations for insulating the police from political pressures and influence. The Commission, *inter alia*, recommended the following:

1. To remove the proverbial Damocles' sword of transfer constantly dangling on the head of the Chief of the Police and assuring him a statutory tenure after proper and careful selection.

2. Constitution of the State Security Committee to help the state government to effectively discharge its superintending responsibility.
3. Insulate the investigation wing of the police from external pressures to ensure its freedom in operational areas of police investigation.

The reports of the National Police Commission are gathering dust. One of the former Home Ministers, late Indirajit Gupta, in a letter to Chief Ministers (April 3, 1997) strongly pressed for police reforms and said that deficiencies in the functioning of the police in our country had arisen largely due to the 'overdose of unhealthy political interference at various levels—misuse of police for political purposes and political patronage quite often extended to the corrupt police personnel'. He drew a blank from the Chief Ministers. Incidentally, Pakistan has stolen a march over India by introducing major reforms in police organisation and structures with a view to depoliticising it. Pakistan has freed their police from political control by enacting Pakistan Police Ordinance, 2001.

It is a known fact that during the peak period of communal riots in Gujarat, the police and the civil administration remained passive and often partisan. The anti-socials and criminals had a field day. The Chairman of the National Human Rights Commission has also deplored the failure of the state to protect 'life, liberty, equality and dignity of the people of Gujarat'. The National Human Rights Commission debunked the claim of the state government that the communal flame was doused within 72 hours. Further, some of the upright police officers who stood their ground and acted firmly and opened fire on the trouble-makers were later on victimised and transferred. Nothing can have a more unsettling impact on the morale of the force.

Gill's success hinges upon the political support he can get from the Chief Minister and his other colleagues. He has already made is presence felt and imparted some drive and dynamism to the police administration. But the task before him is a daunting one.

First, he will have to restore the confidence of the people, and particularly the minority community, in the impartiality of the force and its capacity to function in a non-partisan manner.

Second, young and capable officers have to be posted in the communally sensitive areas and they should be given a free hand in dealing with the criminals and anti-socials. In my long years of service in the police, I have seen that though communal riots may be caused by a number of factors over which the police have no control, the failure of the police to act quickly and effectively causes escalation and extension of the riots and heavy loss of human lives and properties. Though the police use fire arms as a last resort in dealing with unlawful associations, there should be no hesitation during communal riots to open effective fire at the first instance to break up a riotous mob and failure to do, should be viewed as a grave dereliction of the duty on the part of the officers concerned.

Third, investigation of serious and heinous crimes committed during the communal riots has to be done vigorously and followed up by determined prosecution of the offenders. Specific time schedules should be fixed for expeditious completion of investigations. Though the National Human Rights Commission has recommended entrusting of certain critical cases to CBI, it is doubtful if the state government will agree to this. In that event, special investigating squads under the state CID comprising officers of proven integrity and impartiality should be set up for investigation of these cases. Withdrawal from trial of cases occurring during the communal riots by state governments with a view to promoting communal harmony often proves illusory and has to be discouraged.

Fourth, during investigation the police with the help of NGOs should assess extent of damages suffered by the victims and help the administration in making payment of compensation to the affected persons. Fifth, deterrent action has to be taken against the officers for gross omissions and dereliction of duties, and by the same token the officers who have performed the duties well should be commended. Sixth, there should be conscious endeavour to improve minority representation in the force. The composition of the force should reflect the general mix of the communities as it exists in society and make the police set-up more balanced and composite. Reservation of posts for minority groups on the basis of their share of the population is unsound as it will fragment the force on caste and communal lines, but there should be no discrimination against the recruitment of the people from minority communities at any level.

Gill can accomplish these tasks only if he gets full support from the Chief Minister. However, already ominous signals are emanating that the Chief Minister and his Cabinet colleagues are not co-operating with Gill and would be happy to see him out of Gujarat. He has become a thorn in the flesh of many. By handpicking the Ahmedabad Police Commissioner, Gill has sent out signals that he means business, but he cannot accomplish much without political support and backing of the Chief Minister. Hence, chances of qualitative improvement in the functioning of the Gujarat Police are bleak. However, without insulation from political pressures and encouragement of professional leadership, the police will not be able to deal with serious law and order and internal security problems that are likely to erupt again and again. What has happened in Gujarat may also happen in other states if the police function as the minions of the party in power.

—13 June, 2002, The Statesman

5

Use of Handcuffs—Need for a Rational Approach

Arbitrary arrests and misuse of handcuffs are common complaints of abuse of authority against the police. Judicial pronouncements of the Supreme Court in the case of Premshankar Shukla *vs.* Delhi Administration (SC 1980) and Citizens of Democracy *vs.* State of Assam (SC 1996) viewed the existing practice of handcuffing by the police as extremely objectionable and laid down restrictions on the discretion of the police to handcuff the prisoners. The apex court felt that "functional compulsions of security must reach that dismal degree where no alternative will work except manacles".

In the case of Premshankar Shukla, a better class undertrial prisoner in Tihar Jail was required to be taken from the jail house to the magistrate's court and back periodically in connection with certain cases pending against him. The trial court had directed the concerned prison officers that while escorting him to the court or back, handcuffing should not be done, unless it was so warranted. But as the handcuffs were forced on him by the escorts, he sent a telegram to one of the judges of the Supreme Court on the basis of which a *habeas corpus* petition was admitted by the apex court. The Supreme Court speaking through Justice Krishna lyer held that to be consistent with Articles 14 and 19 of the Constitution 'handcuffs must be the last resort as there are other ways of ensuring security. No prisoner shall be fettered routinely or for the convenience of the custodian or escort. The court further laid down that even where in extreme circumstances handcuffs have to be put on the prisoner, the escorting authority "must record contemporaneously the reasons for doing so."

The court was of the view that merely because a person was charged with grave or serious offences, inference of escape did not follow and on that premise alone he could not be handcuffed. Therefore, the court held as arbitrary the provisions of clauses (a), (b), (c) of paras 26:22 of the Punjab Police Manual of routinely handcuffing an undertrial who is accused of a non-bailable offence punishable with three years imprisonment. Further, classification of the under trial prisoners for the purpose of handcuffs into 'better class' or 'ordinary class' as enjoined in the Punjab Police Manual was arbitrary and 'hostile to the constitutional ethos'. In the case of 'Citizens for Democracy', the Supreme Court reiterated its earlier ruling on handcuffing and made its adherence mandatory. The court also emphasised that 'violation and circumvention of the law laid down by the Supreme Court shall attract the provisions of Contempt of Court Act, apart from other penal consequences under the law'.

The Supreme Court's ruling in Premshankar Shukla's case was given in 1980. Only in 1988 (4-10-1988) the Government of India issued the following guidelines regarding handcuffing:

1. No prisoner shall be fettered or handcuffed routinely just because of the convenience of the custodian or escort.
2. It is arbitrary to classify the prisoners for the purpose of handcuffs into 'B' class and ordinary class.
3. Handcuffing should be resorted to in exceptional circumstances where there is clear danger of escaping or where the concerned accused is so violent that he cannot otherwise be secured. Handcuffing may be avoided by increasing the strength of the armed escort or by taking prisoners in a well protected van.

It advised the Home Secretaries and D.Gs. of all state governments to ensure that these instructions were scrupulously observed.

Police Manuals of different states have framed rules incorporating the rulings of the apex court and directions of the Government of India. Andhra Pradesh Police Manual Order No. 461 lays down that undertrial prisoners and accused persons shall not be handcuffed and chained without specific permission of the courts, and whenever it is considered necessary to handcuff certain prisoners while they have been taken out, the written order of the magistrate should be obtained. Permission granted by the magistrate should be maintained in a book to be kept by the guard officer. With regard to handcuffing, a refractory, violent or dangerous prisoner, the officer in charge of the sub-jail guard or the senior police officer present may control him only by utilizing more personnel and by such force as may be necessary, while rushing a messenger to the concerned court or magistrate for permission to handcuff him.

But in practice, the policemen face a number of practical difficulties which should be taken note of. A study done by the Bureau of Police Research and Development (BPR&D) shows that a large number of prisoners have escaped from police custody during the period from 1996-2000. Number of such escapes from some of the major states are as follows:

(*a*) Rajasthan (428)
(*b*) Maharashtra (539)
(*c*) Gujarat (320)
(*d*) Uttar Pradesh (776)
(*e*) West Bengal (106)

However, these statistics do not reveal a complete and clearcut picture without a further specific empirical study to find out as to in how many cases escapes took place precisely because handcuffs were not used. Again during this period, as figures collected by the BPR&D show, that altogether about 4,000 policemen had to face criminal/ departmental action for the escape of the prisoners from their custody. An escape from custody can result in the prosecution of policemen under Section 221 to 225(A) of IPC, which make both intentional and negligent conduct on the part of policemen a cognizable offence. Moreover, police regulations of all states make escape from the custody of the police a serious omission. In such cases, policemen are invariably suspended and disciplinary action is initiated against them. Though the Supreme Court says that use of handcuffs can be minimised by increasing the number of escorts, it becomes in practice very difficult to augment the strength of the escort party, because the available strength at each police station is limited and there has been an exponential increase in the commitments of the police. Again, non-handcuffing of the prisoner in the present scenario poses threats to the security of the police officers. These days not only the terrorists, but also the ordinary criminals carry firearms and do not hesitate to open fire at the law enforcing officials. Sometime back, Vinoy Kumar Jadav, a Sub-Inspector of Delhi Police was shot dead by an accused with criminal antecedents. Undertrials are not docile and submissive and many of them indulge in violent mischievous activities. Further, infrastructure facilities are also inadequate. As the number of jail vans is not enough for the strength of the prisoners, often they are brought in the courts in less secure police vehicles, requiring deployment of more policemen in the escort party. Due to the resource crunch it has become difficult to either augment the police escort strength in each district or add to the number of jail vans.

In countries like U.K. and U.S.A., handcuffing is viewed as one of the accepted practices of the police while effecting arrests and escorting prisoners.

In the U.K. there are case laws on use of handcuffs. Handcuffing is justified when found reasonably necessary in order to prevent an escape [Reed *vs*. Wastie (1972) Crim. L.R. 221].

In another case of 1972, it has been laid down that handcuffing is justifiable where it is reasonably necessary in order to prevent an escape.

Handcuffing is justifiable when found reasonably necessary to terminate a violent breach of the peace by the prisoner [R.V. Lockley (1864), 4F. & F.155]. In Australia, Police Service Handbook of the State of New South Wales provides that the officer is justified in handcuffing prisoners when they have tried to escape or to prevent escape or injury to themselves and others.

In the U.S.A. the Idaho Court of Appeals in an appellate decision declared that a "policy requiring officers to handcuff arrested person when they take him to the jail so that the suspect may not grab a weapon, fight with officers or cause damage to country property is inherently reasonable. Even the most meek-appearing and fragile suspect may have the ability to place the officer, the public and the suspect at great risk".

European Court of Human Rights (ECHR) in interpreting Article 3 of European Human Rights Convention which gives freedom from degrading treatment has laid down that it is in order to restrain a person to effect a lawful arrest or prevent the escape of a person lawfully detained. The court decided in the case of Ranihen *vs*. Finland (1997) that it was not degrading to lead an individual in handcuff past friend and supporters and to keep him handcuffed for a total of two hours in a situation where the use of restraint was necessary.

In the present scenario, with escalating crime and increasing lawlessness, there is an urgent need to review the law on handcuffing the criminals. At present under the existing instruction of the apex court which have the force of law, it is obligatory for the police officer to first make a diary entry at the police station regarding the antecedents of the accused and the reasons as to why it was necessary to handcuff the accused and to produce a copy of the diary entry before the court. It is difficult for the police to comply with these conditions. As a result, the instructions of the Supreme Court are honoured in breach.

Recently, in a national seminar (held on 10th July 2002) in Delhi on the use of handcuffs by the police the well-known lawyer K.T. Tulsi stated that the directions of the Supreme Court were somewhat impractical, based on unrealistic expectations and stem from distrust of the police and this distrust is weakening the foundations of our criminal justice system. It is necessary for the Parliament to pass a comprehensive law on the subject replacing the Prisoners (Attendance in Court) Act and clear up all ambiguities. The law should take into account the operational problems of the police and at the same time contain provisions to prevent misuse of handcuffs by the police. In the case of Premshankar Shukla case, Justice Pathak while giving the concurring judgement significantly observed that " whether handcuffs or other restraint should be imposed on a person is primarily a matter for the decision of the authority responsible for his custody. There is reason for imposing a supervisory regime over the exercise of that decision." The supervisory jurisdiction should perhaps be left with the senior officers of the police. If the enactment of the new law takes long time, a larger Bench of the Supreme Court may be moved to review its decision and observations in the light of the ground realities and practical difficulties faced by the police to implement the directions of the court.

—18 August, 2002, The Statesman

6

Police Encounters : Extra Legal Methods Not the Remedy

The shoot-out at Ansal Plaza has embroiled the Delhi Police in an unseemly but avoidable controversy. The key witness Hare Krishna has alleged that it was not a genuine, but a stage managed encounter—in which two so-called terrorists were killed in cold blood by the Police. Based on the version of Hare Krishna, journalist and Member of Rajya Sabha, Kuldip Nayar, filed a petition before the National Human Rights Commission which, in turn, issued a notice to the Delhi Police to explain their action and also provide protection to Hare Krishna, who was apprehending threats to his life.

Hare Krishna, *prima facie*, appears to be an unreliable witness who, according to newspaper reports, repeatedly changed his versions. His antecedents also do not inspire confidence. Anyone with experience in law enforcement knows that the police will never be so moronic as to stage an encounter in a crowded market place. They, if necessary, would have done it in secluded place to avoid public glare and scrutiny. Now post-mortem conducted by the panel of doctors has vindicated police version and confirmed that the militants died from bullet injuries sustained during encounter. Presence of gunpowder from militants' fingers also indicated that there had been an encounter between the police party and the militants.

Many feel that NHRC's issue of notice to the Delhi Police

will have the effect of demoralising the police and dampening their enthusiasm. This may not be a correct view. From my experience in the NHRC as the Director General (Investigation), I may mention here that if a petition comes to the NHRC from a Member of the Rajya Sabha casting serious doubts on police version in a sensational case, the NHRC has no option but to seek explanation from the police regarding the nature and sequence of events. It cannot remain quiet. The police may feel miffed, but it is unavoidable in a democratic society where the police have to be accountable to multiple mechanisms. But the fact also remains that some sections of the press and some human rights activists have been unnecessarily critical of the police and totally unappreciative of the delicate and dangerous job they are performing in their fight against the terrorists. Every year nearly 700 policemen in India die with their boots on. In no other democratic country so many policemen are killed in their line of duty.

Ansal Plaza shooting also raises the wider issue of police encounters. It cannot be gainsaid that along with genuine there are also fake and stage-managed encounters. Whenever dreaded criminals and terrorists are apprehended, there is tremendous pressure on the police to liquidate them by showing encounters, because their chances of conviction in courts of law are slender. Cases will drag on interminably and witnesses out of fear will not come forward to depose. There is thus also tacit public approval behind police encounter. Civil libertarians presume that all extra-judicial killing stem from blood thirstiness of the police. This is not the case. The police are encouraged to do the dirty work of the society, because the criminal justice system is not functioning and overhauling of the entire system of the administration of justice is too big a task. The fact of the matter is that encounters are not the problem, but merely symptoms of the collapsing system of justice and of the public demand for quick solutions to the law and order problems.

However, for efficient functioning of the police, it is necessary for senior police leaders to resist pressure, for ruthless counter-measures coming from the members of the public and the political masters. They have to discourage sternly shortcut extra-legal methods, and particularly fake encounters. The National Police Commission in its report [Fifth Report of the National Police Commission] recommended that fake encounters had to be discouraged by the police leaders as this is not the remedy for the situation. Answer is to strengthen law and the legal process.

The police and the security personnel when attacked by the terrorists can always exercise their right of private defence. Genuine encounters for the purpose of dealing with the dangerous criminals and the terrorists, can come about within the framework of law with reference to Sections 97, 100 and 103 of IPC which deal with the right of private defence of life and property. Section 46 (3) of the Cr.P.C. empowers the police to use force to the extent of causing death to a person accused of an offence punishable with death or imprisonment for life, if such a person rersists arrest or attempts to evade arrest. Legal provision exists to justify use of force against the criminals and terrorists which may even result in causing their death. Thus an encounter *per se* is neither illegal nor undesirable.

Unfortunately, many fake encounters also do take place. The National Human Rights Commission on receiving complaints of false encounters from Andhra Pradesh Civil Liberties Committee (APCLC) regarding false encounters staged by Andhra police held public hearings in Hyderabad and recorded evidence. The Chairman of the NHRC in his letter dated March 29, 1997, to the Chief Ministers requested them to issue directions through the Directors General of Police to all police stations on the procedures that should be followed in regard to cases where death has been caused in encounters with the police. The Commission felt that the right of private defence should not be manipulated to justify fake encounters, and the procedures of Section 46(3) of the Criminal Procedure Code not be subverted to such an end. In the procedure outlined by the NHRC, it was laid down that in the case of an encounter in which the police are involved, information should be recorded in the police station and if it is considered sufficient to suspect the Commission of a cognizable offence, immediate steps should be taken to investigate the facts and circumstances leading to death and also to ascertain how the offence was committed and by whom. If police officers belonging to the same Police Stations are the members of the encounter party, it is appropriate that the cases are made over for investigation to some other independent investigating agency such as state CID. The procedure outlined by the Commission remains on paper and not being acted on by the state police forces. It is not known what steps the NHRC has taken to enforce them. The upshot is that even genuine police encounters are being viewed with suspicion. Tough counter-measures involving human rights violations are now being loudly advocated against the criminals and terrorists who have no respect for human rights. Recently the Prime Minister in an international gathering of the human right activists said that in the war against terror tough decisions entailing temporary infringement of human rights and freedom were inescapable. There is, however, a danger inherent in it. The danger is that the practice of policing to break law in the name of law-enforcement will be arbitrary as a process and random in its effect. Further, violating the rule of law will have the effect of "scapegoating" the police. Police officers, and particularly the police leaders, have to remember that when the police take recourse to extra-legal tactics to make up for deficiencies of law and legal procedures, they are trying to remedy the inadequacies that they did not create. By resorting to illegal methods and exceeding their mandate they not only take responsibility for crime on themselves but deflect attention to themselves away from the negligence of others. Again, serious violation of the rule of law, when discovered, invites outside interventions and the police organisations in trying to fend off, such interventions develop a "bunker mentality"and become less willing to be transparent and open. It has been aptly said by an American scholar, Dr. David Bayley, that "illegality in the service of public safety makes policing a furtive and anxious activity and undermines pride which is the basis of job satisfaction". And the most effective means for changing the mindset of the police officers will be to convince the police leaders that violating the rule of law is not a sound law-enforcement. They should be encouraged and emboldened to change the moral tone and management priorities within the organisation to convince the rank and file that extra legal methods are counter-productive.

—19 November, 2002, The Statesman

7

Indian Police: Vision for the Future

India attained independence in 1947 and became a sovereign democratic republic on January 26, 1950. Fifty-six years have rolled by since the attainment of country's independence—fulfilment of its 'tryst with destiny'. During this period the country has made rapid strides in many spheres. Democracy, contrary to the views of many Jeremiahs, not only survived but grew in strength in stark contrast to the experience of many countries which became independent almost at the same time. However, though there had been commendable progress in many directions, in the sphere of few enforcement there had been an unfortunate decline, which in turn had impaired good governance and weakened our democratic polity.

For this decline in the quality and standard of law enforcement, often the police, as the most important component of the criminal justice system, is held accountable. Indeed, in democratic countries all over the world, there is a crisis about public safety and in the heart of the crisis is the police who promises to protect the citizens but does not appear to be able to do so. In Indian context, this criticism of the police, though not entirely unmerited, is somewhat simplistic and does not take note of its structural and systemic problems. Indian police till now is governed by the Police Act of 1861, which was passed by the British rulers on the recommendations of the Police Commission of 1860. The Commission of 1860 observed that the organised police as proposed by them would be 'politically useful'. Hence, a ruler-appointed police was set up in India to act as the defender of the establishment. Unfortunately, even after independence the ruler-supportive character of the Indian police did not change and the same system created by the Police Act of 1861 continued. The control mechanism of the British Raj survived. The police remained alienated from the public and continued to be viewed as a coercive long arm of the government that punishes and does not befriend.

Police Reforms

A number of police commissions, set up by different state governments in the sixties of the last century, made a slew of recommendations for strengthening and reorganizing the police. Some of them were implemented and many left in cold storage. The National Police Commission (1978-80), appointed by the Central Government under the chairmanship of the distinguished civil servant Dharam Vira, went into the heart of the matter and along with other reforms of police management and organisation recommended establishment of some institutional mechanisms to insulate the police from extraneous influence and pressure. It felt that without internal autonomy and accountability to law, it would not be possible for the police to function effectively and safeguard the rights of the people. The National Human Rights Commission also endorsed the core recommendations of the National Police Commission and felt that there was a yearning in the country for an "upright police force functioning with propriety and fairness which can be relied on to protect the rights of the citizens". The National Human Rights Commission further impleaded itself in public interest litigation before the Supreme Court asking the apex court to issue directions to the central and state governments for implementation of the recommendations of the National Police Commission. Final decision in the matter now rests with the Supreme Court.

However, for facing the challenges of tomorrow police leaders besides pressing for statutory reforms, will have to initiate a series of steps for qualitative improvement in police work and to streamline the organisational structure and bridge the gap between the police and the community. There is enormous scope for in-house innovative reforms and changes.

Today the problems of law enforcement and order maintenance in the country have become difficult and complex with escalating crime, ever-increasing violence, falling rates of conviction and growing criminalisation of the political system. Rot in the criminal justice system is undermining good governance. The police is getting outgunned by circumstances beyond its control and not able to cope adequately with law and order and crime problems, with its limited resources. In this kind of complex situation, the police necessarily will have to increasingly rely on public support and help for maintenance of order and safety. The public has to be viewed as co-producers with the police of safety and order and here lies the importance and relevance of community policing.

Community Policing

Community policing emerged in 1970s and 1980s in the USA and some of the advanced Western countries when the police realized that the professional and bureaucratic model of policing with the emphasis on up-to-date technology in police work was lessening police contact with the public and not reducing crime. Officers were losing touch with the community they were meant to serve. Community-oriented policing seeks to break down the anonymity of the police and diminish the psychological distance between the police and the public. It puts faces into uniforms and allows the community to know the police in human terms.

There is often the facile assumption that the community policing assumes that the public wants partnership with the police. Very often there is a feeling in the community that they have all heard it before. There is also fear of the public that they will face reprisals from the criminals if they cooperate with the police. To win community's confidence, the police will have to demonstrate that it sincerely seeks community's help in combating crime and disorder and the public can repose confidence in it. Sir Robert Bunyard, a well-known British police officer, said, "to gain public confidence we want to see the police force as friends, and one of the key things about friends is that we can trust them".

Experts on crime including the police understand well that crime cannot be prevented only through law enforcement. The capacity of the police to reduce and control crime is very much limited by social and economic forces over which it has no control. And many thinking police officers rightly complain that they are expected to protect the communities from the consequences of their own neglect. Crime is the outcome of complex social and biological conditions and its prevention must involve rigorous analysis and interventions into those conditions. For meaningful crime prevention, the police role has to be transformed. The range of police activity has to expand from narrow boundaries of law enforcement and the police has to become engaged in advocating solutions to social problems at several levels of the government. "So the police, once regarded as the defenders of the *status quo*, has become the last best hope for those who want progressive ameliorative, grass roots social changes".[1]

Further, the police leaders and administrators will have to think of developing new proactive strategies to enable the police to play an effective role in the new century with its myriads of challenges and possibilities. They will have to re-evaluate core strategies, organisational structures, management practices, occupational culture and democratic accountability. Some important organisational changes and management reforms are required.

1. David Baley (*Police for the Future*).

First, there should be well-planned concrete efforts to upgrade the quality and skill of the constables or reduce their number in favour of those who will be more useful. Ill-motivated and ill-trained constabulary constituting nearly 80 per cent of the force continues to remain the Achilles heel of the Indian police. The Police Commission of 1902, set up by Lord Curzon, categorically stated, "Constables are not the suitable agency for the performance of important duties assigned to them... The duties of the constables should not be above his class." Majority of the constables retire in the same rank without any promotion. The National Police Commission recommended that the promotional structure within the police system should be radically revised to permit smooth and quick promotional flow from the rank of constables. However, even two decades after publication of the NPC's report, no meaningful steps have been taken for empowerment of the constables and improving their career prospects. Unless the constables move ahead from the predominantly mechanical role assigned to them, the cutting edge of the police administration will remain blunted.

Second, police officers, particularly police leaders, will have to cultivate greater professionalism. Professionalism implies acquisition of certain skills and expertise by the members of the profession and constant efforts on their part to refine and improve their skills. For this erosion of professionalism, senior police officers must accept their shares of responsibility. They tend to forget that professionalism should be the hallmark of the police leaders in the coming years. In the new management style of tomorrow the role of the supervisors as controllers will lessen but as group motivators and agents of change will increase.

Third, there must be decentralization of the command structure. Though police is a hierarchical and centralised organisation, discretion increases as one goes down the line. Very often considerable discretion is exercised by the subordinates working alone and making decisions hastily.

The police work is thus beset with a fundamental paradox. Police organisation allows discretion in practice while, at the same time, maintaining top-down command system. The formal and informal structures of authority in policing are not congruent. The British Audit Commission (1991), in a radical proposal for decentralization, recommended that the decision about the needs and strategies should be made by the commanders of the Basic Police Units (BPUs). At present, these decisions are monopolized by Police Headquarters.

Fourth, there should be manpower audit and increasing use of the civilians in the non-enforcement jobs of the police. In many countries, civilians are now replacing police officers at about half the cost. At present over 30 per cent in Britain and 27 per cent in the USA police employees are civilians. They have taken over administrative chores like report writing, data entering and other non-enforcement jobs from the operational police officers.

Fifth, police must take notice of the new trends towards privatization of the police service. Indeed, this has become a global phenomenon. In the USA, in 1990, private security employed two and half-times as many people as police personnel. The phenomenal growth of private security clearly shows that the public is not expecting police officers to deal with all kinds of situations and crimes. In India, there is a lot of scope for partnership between the police and private security agencies. They should not be seen as mutually exclusive.

These in-house reforms have to be supplemented by enlightened political will to improve policing in the country. On the eve of country's independence, Jawaharlal Nehru said of the 'great triumphs and achievements that await us'. However, triumphs and achievements will continue to wait unless the quality and standard of law enforcement improves and a new professional and people-friendly police is built up. There cannot be social and economic progress in a chaos.

8

Scourge of Corruption and Strategies to Combat it

For a developing country like India, corruption is a scourge. It is anti-national, anti-poor, inequitable and also seriously retards a country's economic development. However, in the 1970s, many economists had argued that corruption sometimes enabled entrepreneurs to bye-pass cumbersome government regulations and thus helped the process of development. Samuel P. Huntington* bluntly stated that in terms of economic growth the only thing worse than a rigid-over-centralized dishonest bureaucracy was a rigid, over-centralized and honest bureaucracy. Some others held that corruption could also have a desirable distributive impact, and it shifted income and wealth from richer individuals and companies to the poorer ones. These arguments, which are advanced in support of corruption at micro level, are fallacious from the macro point of view. Corruption, even when petty and routine, cannot be a means of optimizing allocation of resources, stimulating economic growth and improving living standards. It causes illegal transfer of state revenue to richer and influential private individuals who are in a position to pay bribes to the detriment of those who cannot. Indeed, the evil effects of corruption far outweigh are so-called benefits. The UNDP Report on 'Human Development in South Asia 1999—the Crisis of Governance' says that if corruption levels in India were reduced to those

* Huntington, Samuel, P., *Order Interchanging Societies.*

of the Scandinavian countries, investment in the country would increase annually by 10 per cent and GDP growth by 1.5 per cent. It is sometimes argued that corruption and bribery are necessary lubricants for the cumbersome system of administration. But this grease-the-wheel argument is flawed. Speed money often slows down the pace of administration further.

The Santhanam Committee in its report on 'Prevention of Corruption' has argued that corrupt officials, instead of speeding up, actually cause administrative delays, in order to obtain bribes. Sometimes, even the payment of bribe does not help because there is a multiple veto power system in operation. A high official in Delhi reportedly told a friend that if he wants him to move a file, he is not sure if he can be of help. But if he wants him to stop a file, he can do it immediately. This ability 'to stop file fast' at multiple points (often installed to keep corrupt officials at check) may increase inefficiency as well as corruption. Paolo Mauro*, in his study 'Corruption and Growth', has established the negative relationship between corruption and economic growth for a number of developing countries. It is sometimes difficult to assess the indirect costs of corruption, but frequently they exceed the direct cost. Sometimes, valuable resources are wasted on projects that may yield opportunities for substantial grafts. In consequence, sectors favouring socio-economic development such as health, housing and education suffer.

Corruption also hampers entrepreneurship and intellectual pursuits. Many bright persons, instead of following the straight path, try to explore ways and means of 'getting around the system'. They feel that it is not necessary to waste time and effort in developing a business career when one can enjoy large income from cut money in a suitable government employment.

---

* Paolo Mauro, 'Corruption and Growth', *Quarterly Journal of Economic*, August 1995. Why worry about corruption? *IMF Economic Issues 6*, Washington DC, February 1997.

Deregulation

It is sometimes argued that deregulation and privatization are the panacea for corruption. This is not a fact. Experience in countries like Russia, China and India have shown that deregulation sometimes can lead to an increase in corruption. Abrupt deregulation of a number of economic activities can widen the scope for corruption. If there is no reasonably powerful regulatory mechanism, opportunities for grafts can multiply. In many cases corrupt rulers may be keen to privatize state assets because of the opportunity of large one-time gains. Privatization in developing countries provides many examples of selling of state assets far below the market level prices.

Again, efforts to avoid punishment and detection make corruption very disruptive. Corrupt officials will try to induce investment and transactions in the direction of lower detection activities. Bureaucrats in poor countries often opt for import of complex technology of goods (where detecting improper valuation or over-invoicing is difficult) in preference to more standardized appropriate technology of goods. They will prefer allocation of government funds in a few large defence contracts to spending the money in building health clinics or schools.

Corruption Perception Index

Turning to situation in India, one notes with dismay that it has become one of the most corrupt countries in the world. Transparency International's Corruption Perception Index (CPI), 2002 ranks 102 countries in terms of the degree to which corruption is perceived to exist among public officials and politicians. Of the 102 countries surveyed, India ranks 71. TI's survey of international business perception ranks India worse than China. However, it has to be borne in mind that corruption perception index is a study based upon the perception of business people and the risk analysts. It is not based on hard data, but it does present an overall view.

Typology of Corruption

In India, as well as in many other countries of South Asia, corruption can be divided into three categories, namely, petty, middling or grand. There is a growing perception that in India, corruption has moved upwards from petty corruption in the 60s and 70s to the highest levels of the State in 1980s and 1990s. This is a very ominous development because corruption at the top distorts fundamental decisions about development priorities and policies and projects. In advanced industrial countries, these core decisions are taken through transparent competition and merit, even though petty corruption may occur downstream.

Today, in the country, corruption has become so widespread and all-pervasive that there is a growing feeling amongst the people that it has become too well-entrenched, and it is not possible to get out of the corruption trap. Countries like France, in nineteenth century, Singapore and Hongkong, in the twentieth century have completed the transition from high corruption society to low corruption ones. Strong political will and commitment to a clear anti-corruption agenda can bring about similar encouraging outcome in India.

Anti-Corruption Strategies

Some of the strategies to combat corruption effectively can be worked out and prioritised. First, there is need for setting up of powerful and effective institutional mechanisms to curb corruption. In Hongkong, the Independent Commission Against Corruption (ICAC) has done remarkable job in reducing corruption. The ICAC was given the power to investigate and prosecute cases of corruption and also to engage in a campaign of public education. The government indicated its commitment by appointing a person of unimpeachable integrity to head the ICAC and by prosecuting some big fishes. Unfortunately, in India, the big fishes are seldom fried. Very often, corrupt persons prove too powerful and influential to be brought to book.

Second, corruption can be reduced considerably by scrapping many obsolete and archaic laws and rationalising the remaining ones. There are laws and rules in existence, which perpetuate corruption and give opportunities for corrupt practices. There license, permit, quota-regime continues even after liberalization and globalization of 1991. There are about 3,000 central statutes and numerous state statutes and laws with several exemption clauses and discretionary powers. For instance, it requires nearly 47 different approvals to construct a building in Mumbai and a small-scale entrepreneur has to handle 32 different inspectors and 46 different documents. These are breeding grounds of corruption.

Third, an effective Right to Information Bill will go a long way to help the citizens to combat corruption. In India, the Right to Information Bill is lying with the Parliament for several decades. At present, the public has only limited access to details of financial and administrative transactions. In developed countries like the USA and the UK, people have the right to access to papers and documents except, those pertaining to the security of the State and matters relating to defence. People's right to information will make government policies and programmes more transparent and will be an effective antidote to corruption.

Fourth, it will be necessary and useful to have Public Interest Disclosure Act. Several Western countries, to fight corruption and mal-administration, have enacted Public Interest Disclosure Acts, which are called Whistle-Blower Acts. Similar laws can be enacted in India to ensure that informants are protected against retribution or any form of discrimination for reporting what they perceive to be wrong doing, which may ultimately turn out to be not entirely or substantially true.

---

*Controlling Corruption,—Robert Khitgard.

Robert Klitgard* devised the formula that lies at the heart of the corruption problem. It equals corruption with monopoly power plus discretion minus accountability. Corruption takes place when a person has monopoly over goods and services and has discretion to decide who will receive and how much and is not accountable.

Fifth, swift punishment of the corrupt public servants and confiscation of property derived from crime are two instruments that can produce a visible impact. A time period has to be fixed for trial of corruption cases. In big corruption cases, long duration of trials results in acquittals for multiple reasons and thus making corruption a low risk and high-profit business. There should also be a mechanism to identify the corrupt public servants without disclosing their names publicly. At present, there is a mechanism to do that but is confined to lower rank officials only. A provision in the Prevention of Corruption Act should enable drawal of list of such public servants without inviting legal complications. Again, Benami Transaction Prohibition Act, 1988 was enacted to penalise public servants who dishonestly acquire ill-gotten money. But this provision under Section 5 of the Act can be implemented if rules are made under Section 8 by prescribing authority and laying down the manner and the procedure of acquiring Benami property by the States. Such rules inexplicably have not been framed yet. The National Commission to Review the Working of the Constitution has recommended that the Union Government without any further loss of time should frame rules under Section 8 of the Act for acquiring Benami property.

The present perception that the responsibility of eradicating corruption is that of the government alone is erroneous. In view of the extent and magnitude of corruption, the government alone cannot eradicate corruption. The people and civil society institutions have also to play an active role in these cleansing campaigns. A time has come to involve responsible and public-spirited citizens to create an awareness in the society about the menace of corruption and seek their help and advice in combating it. Such an initiative is unlikely to come from the public. A beginning may be made by the vigilance organisations by forming core groups of citizens of unimpeachable integrity to act as watchdogs on expenditure of public funds in respect of various development programmes. Some tentative steps taken in this direction by N. Vittal, former Central Vigilance Commissioner, though well-meant, could not be sustained. Agencies such as the Hongkong's Independent Commission Against Corruption (ICAC) have established formal arrangements whereby public participation in policy formulation is ensured.

Unfortunately, is India, anti-corruption wings in different states have become politicised and very often utilised for political witch-hunts rather than preventing political corruption. In some states, it has become an accepted practice to start criminal cases against political opponents when a new party comes to power. Unfortunately, the cases are not taken to the logical end in the shape of regular investigation and submission of chargesheets in the court of law and speedy trial. Ultimately, nothing happens and none is brought to book. Only the well-known politicians stand tarnished and develop a totally cynical attitude to the problem of corruption.

Corruption in judiciary is another problem, which is not very often discussed because of the Contempt of Courts Act. The National Commission to Review the Working of the Constitution has suggested appropriate changes in the law, and even a constitutional amendment, enabling citizens to use the rights of freedom of speech in presenting the truth without fear of contempt. Today, charges of misconduct against some senior judges have sullied the image of judiciary and it is necessary for the government and the legal fraternity to devise some urgent corrective steps.

—10/11 March, 2003, The Statesman

9

The Rot Within

Arrest of R.K. Sharma, the former Mumbai Police Commissioner, in the Telgi Scam has opened a can of worms. Investigation by a Special Investigation Team has unearthed the Mumbai Police's linkage, both at the senior and junior levels, but especially at the top, with the criminals — a discovery that has sullied the reputation of the police force beyond repair.

In a hierarchical organisation like the police, the head of the force occupies a pivotal and unique position. By his exemplary conduct and professional competence he is supposed to inspire his subordinates and win the confidence of the public. The Indian police has been fortunate in having a number of such leaders. The Mumbai police also had some distinguished commissioners who have displayed leadership of a high order. But there is no doubt that a man of doubtful integrity can wreak havoc and vitiate the atmosphere within the force.

A Director General or Commissioner of Police has to be selected with utmost care. The reputation, good or bad, of officers is hardly a secret and the exclusion of corrupt officers is not a difficult task. Unfortunately, selection of the Directors General or Commissioners of Police is increasingly becoming the prerogative of political masters who are not interested in an officer's individual merit. Honest and upright officers are considered inflexible and therefore sidelined.

Section 3 of the Police Act, 1861 — passed by the British after the Sepoy Mutiny — which still governs the structure and working of the Indian police, lays down that the superintendence of the Police shall vest in the state government. But in the name of "superintendence", complete political control over the police is now exercised by the party in power. In each state, there are three or four officers of the same rank as Director General of Police. If the head of the police proves intransigent, he is quickly replaced by another officer, of the same rank, who *kowtows* to the party in power. Indeed, supervision in the name of democracy has eroded the foundations on which the criminal justice system rests.

Not only in the selection of the chief of the police, but also in the transfer and posting of all important police functionaries, there is now constant extraneous interference. This has encouraged the police personnel to believe that their career advancement does not depend on their professional performance but on being able to curry favour with politicians who matter. Politicking and hobnobbing with politicians have become important occupations for an average police officer. Needless to say, the chain of command and control has been severely weakened. Moreover the nexus with politicians has eroded accountability and further encouraged corruption. The last is most worrisome because corruption in the police imperils the right to life and liberty of citizens and encourages criminality.

To restore the credibility of the police, the National Police Commission recommended that the chief of police in a state has to be assured of a statutory tenure in office without the Damocles' sword of transfer hanging over his head all the time. A secure tenure will strengthen his hands in the face of irregular pulls and pressures. The period of tenure would have to be included in specific provisions of the Police Act itself. The Commission also recommended that the police chief be selected from a panel prepared by a committee headed by the Chairman of the Union Public Service Commission, and other Members including the Chief Secretary of the State and the existing police chief. The removal of the police chief before the expiry of his term would require the approval of the State Security Commission, an institution recommended by the National Police Commission, to help the State government in discharging its superintending responsibility in an open manner. However, these recommendations of the Commission have been kept in the cold storage by both the Central and State governments.

The National Police Commission had also recommended that corrupt officers be weeded out by invoking Article 311(2)(c) of the Indian Constitution. Clause (c) in the Article had to be amended to allow the President or the Governor to take such summary measures in the interest of not only the security of the state but also maintenance of the integrity of people in public service.

The problem of political interference in the working of the police is not only unique to India but is common to other democratic countries as well. The United States of America tried to deal with it by strengthening the position of the police chiefs by giving them a reasonable tenure of office, by reducing political interference, and by laying emphasis on high admission standards. In the United Kingdom too, the need to prevent political patronage from affecting the performance of civil services was recognized by the creation of the Civil Services Commission in 1855. This established an independent civil service through open competition. It, however, took 15 years for political parties to relinquish the patronage they had enjoyed till then and agree to the new arrangement.

The KNAPP Commission (1971), investigating police corruption in New York City, classified corrupt policemen into two categories — meat-eaters and grass-eaters. The meat-eaters are policemen who aggressively misuse police powers for personal gain. The grass-eaters accept the pay-offs that police work occasionally throws their way. Although the meat-eaters get huge payoffs and make headlines, yet they represent a small percentage of corrupt policemen. Meat-eaters however get a boost when they get a venal police chief, who can exercise no control over them. They become exploitative and predatory to the extreme.

This is precisely what happened in Mumbai. Politicians in Maharashtra responsible for backing an unsuitable police chief have done a great disservice not only to the Mumbai police but to the country as well. In an organisation like the police where opportunities and temptations are many, the police chiefs have to be scrupulously fair and honest. To quote a veteran Police Chief Patric Murphy, *"except your pay cheque there is no such thing as a clean buck."*

So far, the SIT has done painstaking investigation and unravelled omissions and commissions of the Commissioner of Police and other police personnel, who have amassed huge properties and shielded Abdul Karim Telgi and his gang. Internal investigation is however sometimes more useful because officers within the organisation at times tend to close ranks and refuse to blow the whistle when investigation is being done by an outside agency.

The Telgi scam undoubtedly has other dimensions. It has inter-state ramifications and there is every likelihood that politicians who favoured Telgi also instructed police officers to shield him. It is doubtful how far the Central Bureau of Investigation will be able to carry on vigorous investigation against these bigwigs who operate from behind the scene. Whatever the fallout, the investigation has to be followed up by prosecution and deterrent punishment to the criminals and their patrons.

—23 December 2003, The Telegraph

SECTION II

Cross Border Terrorism

10

Jehadi Groups : Principal-Agent Problem in Pakistan

General Pervez Musharraf's admonition to the rabid Islamic clerics as well as the militant outfits operating in Pakistan for making irresponsible statements and aggravating tension between India and Pakistan highlights the problem that Pakistan is facing in dealing with these groups. This has been described as a typical principal-agent problem: the interest of Pakistan (the principal), as Jessica Stern mentions in an article published in the journal, *Foreign Affairs,* and those of the militant groups (the agent) are not fully aligned. The militant groups, who are called 'freedom fighters' in Pakistan, operating in Kashmir and engaged in acts of terrorist violence have kept a big chunk of the Indian army and para military forces tied down there. For Pakistan, this is a cost-effective proxy war. Unable to mount a serious conventional military challenge, it has looked on terrorism as an alternative strategy. According to one estimate, about 3000 to 4000 *mujahideens* operating in Kashmir at any given time have kept engaged more than 300,000 Indian security personnel. This definitely keeps India off balance and Pakistan rulers had hoped that through this 'surrogate warfare', it would be able to liberate Kashmir and also dismember India. These Islamic militant jehadi groups not only fight against the Indian Army, but also indulge in murder, rape and other acts of brutal terrorism in complete violation of international norms. Their activities damage

Pakistan's fragile international reputation and confirm the growing international perception that it has become a terrorist state. Again, many of these mujahideens are also getting involved in bitter sectarian conflicts raging inside Pakistan.

However, prospects of Pakistan successfully reining in these militant groups are not very bright. Pakistan trained and financed these irregulars with a view to keeping India off balance, and bleeding it white, but in the process, it has now created a Frankenstein monster that threatens to devour Pakistan's society. Due to a number of reasons, these groups are growing in size and strength and developing a vested interest in the continuation and prolongation of the jehad against India. First, many of these militant groups have acquired vast funds. The view that use of terror is poor man's method of waging war is no longer valid. These groups receive huge donations from the sympathetic Wahhabis in Saudi Arabia and other Gulf countries and members of Pakistani diaspora. It is reported that Laskar-e-Toiba (Army of the Pure) and its parent organisation, Markaz ad Dawa-Irshad, have raised so much money that they are planning to open their own bank. Top leaders of the militant groups live well and receive good salaries as well as many other facilities. Even the operators in the field receive bonuses for successful missions. In a poor country like Pakistan, joining the militant groups is not an unattractive proposition. Thus, as the so-called *jehad* movement has acquired its financial momentum; it will be increasingly difficult for the Pakistani authorities to close the show and crack down on these groups even if it intends to do so. There are now entrenched interests to support the present situation and prolong the war in Kashmir. As long as 'Jehad International Inc' remains profitable, says a Pakistan scholar, those with financial interests in the war will work to prolong it. Second, many fundamentalist groups have become addicted to jehad and they cannot leave it. Perhaps, even if the Kashmir problem is solved, fundamentalist groups will not keep quiet. They will create problems in Pakistan and seek to set up there some kind of a Taliban style regime. Third, it is becoming increasingly difficult to exercise control over the criminals and lumpen elements who have swelled the ranks of the militants. Initially, they were hired by the terrorist groups to do their dirty work. These criminals carry out wanton acts of violence and are not committed to the militant groups' goals and ideals. They are criminals and not crusaders. Infiltration of these criminal elements has further compounded the principal-agent problem for Pakistan. Fourth, many of these groups are in possession of enormous arms and explosives. Deweaponisation programmes of the Federal and Provincial governments in Pakistan have achieved little success. The obvious hard nuts to crack will be the tribal areas which serve as the originating points of the illegal arms and from where dealers obtain deliveries of arms for their clients in the cities. Darra Adam Khel, located in the tribal area south of Peshawar, has become the largest centre for manufacture of arms in Pakistan. Here, factories were developed during the Afghan war against Soviet Russia, but though the war came to an end in 1989, the facilities have since doubled and the business continues to flourish. The extent of arms proliferation can be realised from the fact that in the North Western Frontier Province of Pakistan alone there are about two million arms licence holders including those for prohibited bore weapons. Earlier attempts of the government to dismantle Darra factories evoked violent reactions from the tribesmen and the authorities had to quietly shelve the deweaponisation programme. Success of Musharraf's deweaponisation programme to reduce the availability of guns to the sectarian gangs and criminals remains doubtful. A big question mark hangs over it.

Further, rabid fundamentalism is spread and sustained by innumerable *madarsas* that have now proliferated in

Pakistan. They preach a narrow and violent version of Islam. Pakistan's military ruler, General Zia-ul-Haque, during his tenure promoted these madarsas with a view to enlisting the support of the religious parties for his rule and also to recruit volunteers in Pakistan for the anti-Soviet war in Afghanistan. In Zia's time many madarsas were financed by the state, giving the government some measure of control over these institutions.

Different Pakistani governments have tried to exercise control over the madarsas without much success. Recently, Pakistan's Interior Minister, Moinuddin Haider announced a reform plan that would require the madarsas to register with the government, disclose their financial resources, obtain permission before admitting foreign students and stop sending students to militant training camps. This plan of reform, however, has met with little success. The madarsas have stubbornly refused to be regulated by the government. It is learnt that only 4,350 of the estimated 50,000 madarsas in Pakistan have registered with the government. Chancellors of many of the madarsas have refused to expand or alter their curricula as suggested by the government, stating that these madarsas were older than Pakistan "having been designed 1200 years ago in Iraq". They deemed the reform plan as "against Islam". The madarsas, which only impart theological instruction and ignore secular subjects, make the students unfit for suitable employment in a modern society and make them ready recruits for the holy war. They go to swell the ranks of the militants. The madarsas are also offering training to students from Burma, Nepal, Bangladesh, Afghanistan, Mongolia and Kuwait. Out of 700 students at the Khudamuddin madarsa, writes Jessica Stern, nearly 127 are foreigners. Some of them proclaim their plans to carry on *jehad* not only in India, but also in the West, which, they think, is being run by the Jews. Several militant groups boast of burning American flags on their calendars and posters.

Operations of the militant groups are also aggravating law and order problems inside Pakistan. They have inflamed the old sectarian war between the Sunnis and the Shias in Pakistan. Their running battle has now become deadly and serious and taken a heavy toll of lives. Iran is reportedly helping and funding the Shia groups who feel discriminated. It helped the formation of 'Tehrik-e-Jafaria-e-Pakistan (TJP) to protect the interests of Pakistan's Shia Muslims. Shia-Sunni conflict has now taken the form of a proxy war between Iran and Saudi Arabia on Pakistan's soil with disastrous impact on law and order and social cohesion in Pakistan. Many of the madarsas issue anti-Shia fatwas and the boys indoctrinated in these institutions are trained to look on the Shias as '*Kafir*'. Military rulers of Pakistan by aiding and abetting 'holy war' in Kashmir and supporting the Taliban regime in Afghanistan are indirectly fanning the flames of sectarianism in Pakistan.

It is possible that General Musharraf really wants to exercise tighter control over the jehadi groups, but the capacity of the military government to do so is becoming increasingly circumscribed. Sometime back, Pakistan's Interior Minister announced the government's resolve to put an end to fund-raising and public display of weapons in the name of jehad. He had to buckle under the combined onslaughts of the militant outfits and was forced to say in a meeting in Islamabad on February 23, 2001 that the government considers Kashmir to be "an unfinished agenda" and would not backtrack on that issue. The military rulers are clearly aware of the threats these jehadi outfits pose to the internal security of Pakistan. America has also scolded Pakistan and asked it to crack down on the militant groups, close the madarsas and threatened to cut off international aid if positive steps are not taken in this regard. But it is doubtful if the Pakistani government will succeed in controlling these groups, or if everybody in the government is really interested in doing so. Now for Pakistan, it is very difficult to exorcise the ghost of jehadi mindset that has developed since the Afghan war. A culture of violence has also taken deep roots. The West fears that conflict between India and Pakistan may further escalate over Kashmir and culminate in a nuclear war. Terrorism and mindless acts of violence of the militants further enhance that risk.

However, on the eve of Musharraf's visit, India has to keep in mind the stark fact that army rule in Pakistan has become a reality that cannot be wished away. There were times for India to make common cause with the democratic forces in Pakistan against the authoritarianism of the army. Now perhaps India should try to make, if possible, a common cause with the army against the terrorism of the jehadi groups. Pakistan's military ruler also understands the mischief potential of these groups and the long-term threats they pose not only to India and Pakistan, but to the entire region. One only hopes that Vajpayee-Musharraf summit will successfully explore the ways and means of gradually neutralising these militant outfits.

—9 July, 2001, The Statesman

11

Chasing the Shadows—Investigations into Terrorist Strikes in America

FBI has launched a comprehensive and wide-ranging investigation to identify the people responsible for the catastrophic air strikes on New York and Washington and also those who planned and masterminded these attacks. In this investigation named as 'Pent Bom' (Pentagon Twin Towers Bombing) nearly four thousands agents and three thousand analysts are involved and this team under the supervision of the Deputy Director of the FBI, Jone Pickard, is working out the numerous clues and leads coming from various sources to unearth this monstrous criminal conspiracy.

FBI has now released the list of 19 young men with their photographs who are believed to be the hijackers. The agency hopes that their pictures will unravel more leads. The surprising thing about these young suicidal terrorists is that most of them were not moronic fanatical zealots who have nothing to look forward in life. Some of them were educated and technically skilled people who could have lived and enjoyed comfortable middle class lives. Some left wives and children behind. Yet they were consumed by an intense hatred for America and an overwhelming urge to do violence to the enemy. Investigation will reveal how and by whom they were recruited and how they prepared themselves over months or years to accomplish their maniacal mission and how carefully nurtured fanaticism overcame their instincts for self-preservation.

However, they were only visible agents of a carefully planned and deep laid conspiracy meticulously worked out by some master minds. They were probably 'sleepers'. In planning terrorist operations, certain individuals are strategically placed as 'sleepers' and activated as and when required during the struggle. Evidence available so far indicates that Mohammad Atta was the ring leader of the 19 hijackers, although some yet unknown and undisclosed persons may have pulled the operation. Bin Laden is the prime suspect. Another suspect is his lieutenant Ayman-al-Zawahri, who was responsible for the assassination of Anwar Sadat in 1981 and also indicted in the 1998 U.S. Embassy bombings, and has also the experience of plotting something of the scale of September 11 attacks.

Tracing the mastermind, who planned the conspiracy, is not an easy job. Infrastructure of the terrorist organisations like Al-Qaida is centrifugal which enhances its tactical flexibility and allows the terrorist groups to operate against the targets at their convenience. This tactical flexibility is of great significance, because of the asymmetrical power relationship between the terrorists and the government they are attacking. In this connection, it may be mentioned that European underground movements, which developed so well during the Second World War, were by any standards vast organisations with rigid and hierarchical structures patterned on military models. In the case of hierarchical organisation, extensive social support is necessary, but a mobile centrifugal infrastructure can function without extensive social support. The organisations are divided into small cells and they devise elaborate anti-infiltration procedures and take steps to ruthlessly weed out agents and informers in their ranks.

Today, a vast amount of intelligence is collected through what is called "technological snooping" with the help of orbiting satellites, long-range cameras and various other detecting instruments. But for centrifugal terrorist organisations, Human Intelligence (Humint) is the most useful source of information and sometimes this is the only information one has to rely on. But then raising a source 'in place' and then handle him successfully is a very difficult, delicate and time-consuming job. Besides finding suitable agents from the ranks of the terrorists, efforts have to be made to infiltrate agents from outside. It is this invaluable source of information that had enabled the FBI to detect the terrorist plot to blow up the Lincoln Tunnel and the United Nations Building. In this case, the FBI was lucky to get such an agent in the terrorist group itself. In America, now criticisms have been voiced against the intelligence outfits with 30 billion dollar annual budget because they had no inkling of the diabolical plot that must have been planned and hatched over a long time. And some intelligence analysts are of the view that this has happened because the CIA shied away from Humint operations which are difficult. Their agents feel far more comfortable with technological things which are clean.

It is known that the members of the Bin Laden's Al-Qaida network keep minimum electronic communications (which the USA is good in intercepting) and they seldom use cell phones. The members of the group are fired with religious fervour and messianic ideology which makes them relatively immune to the lure of lucre. The political goal of Al-Qaida is the creation of an Islamic Caliphate and it has little interest in conventional politics. Because of its distinct religious motivation it can recruit its cadres from anywhere among the disaffected one billion Moslems in the world. Unlike the nationalist terrorists, they are not recruited from a relatively small pool.

For effectively curbing these terrorist outfits, it is necessary to trace out and initiate action against their paymasters. Money is the fuel of terrorism. The belief that the use of terror is the poor man's method of waging war is no longer valid. Various terrorist groups in the world are quite affluent and do not suffer from lack of resources. America now plans to attack terror by shutting down the financial supply lines. Bush administration has now unveiled a list of 13 terrorist groups, 11 individuals and 3 charities whose assets will be frozen by the USA at home and abroad. Some of these organisations are linked to Bin Laden, but others are said to be independent of him, but active in Philippines, Kashmir and elsewhere. Among the charities that come in the list of Bush administration is the Al Rashid, a Muslim charity operating out of Karachi providing financial support to Islamic militants and families of those killed in fighting in Afghanistan, Kashmir and Chechnya. It brings out a newspaper *Dha'rb-i-Munin* that proclaims 'holi war' against Americans and Israelis.

Major Western industrial nations have also now decided to seize the assets of the terrorists. Germany has frozen 13 accounts linked to the Taliban and Bin Laden. Even Pakistan has ordered private banks to seize accounts held by Harkat-ul-Mujaheedin, a terrorist group. This financial crackdown has received a wide measure of support. Nevertheless, it will not be easy to turn off the flow of funds. Bin Laden's money is believed to be scattered among as many as 65 countries, and often it moves out surreptitiously through back-door channels. There is also what is called "reverse money laundering"—clean funds ultimately used for criminal purposes. However, if the flow of funds to the terrorist groups can be cut off, it will indeed make a difference. In Northern Ireland, IRA Group used o receive funds from the money donated by the affluent Irish Americans. An organisation called Irish Northern Aid (NORAID) was set up by Michael Flannery in the eighties to collect funds from the Irish Americans. It was also the main conduit for supply of arms to the IRA. Later, FBI cracked down on the NORAID, resulting in substantial dwindling of the flow of contribution to the IRA from the United States. This decimation of the NORAID to large extent retarded IRA's expansion programme. The successful campaign against NORAID illustrates how the elimination of an organisation's financial resources can have a lasting and direct impact than other forms of counter-terrorism which concentrates more on gun-men and bombers rather than the paymasters. So it is necessary to get at the financial support of the terrorists' networks.

Now with the American air strikes in full blast on Afghan cities, it is very likely that the Al-Qaida of Bin Laden may resort to spectacular acts of violence and destruction against the targets of hostile countries which includes India. This is often done by terrorist organisations to overcome stress and strain within the organisation and with a view to restoring internal cohesion. External violence is used as a means of keeping the members together and the internal problems of organisation often serve as a catalyst for external violence. Today, Bin Laden has become, as Stephen Cohen has written in the *Washington Post*, some sort of 'Ford Foundation of the terrorists'. He is spawning 'privatised terrorism and has nameless faceless cellular networks crouching to spring at the enemy's targets at any suitable time or place.

For India, there is another cause for deep worry. General Musharraf has said that though Pakistan is in alliance with the United States in its campaign in Afghanistan and in its battle against terrorism, it is not going to eschew support for the freedom struggle in Kashmir. It means that Pakistan will not renounce its support for the jehadi groups and we can expect cross-border terrorism. Pakistan's view that terrorism in Kashmir is a legitimate national liberation war and is to be distinguished from any global campaign against terrorism in something that India should carefully take note of. Already, there are demonstrations against Musharraf for backing USA against Taliban. Far more massive protests will take place if he tries to obstruct the jehad in Kashmir. Some Pakistani experts feel that Pakistan may ditch Afghanistan, but it is well nigh impossible to give up its involvement in Kashmir without provoking a civil war.

So India should gear itself to fight its own battle, and be prepared for hard and difficult times. For this purpose, it is necessary to heighten public awareness of the impending terrorist threats and the need to counteract it. The key to success in any terrorist campaign in a democracy is the public sensitised to and aware of terrorist goals and tactics and supportive of anti-terrorist measures by the government.

—20 October, 2001, The Statesman

12

Uncertain Partners—Pak-American Alliance in Afghan Conflict

Mounting civilian casualties as a result of ceaseless American bombing is adding another dimension to the war in Afghanistan. Anglo-American air strikes are no longer targetted and proportional. Innocent civilians are becoming victims of the attack and this loss of civilian lives is slowly, but inexorably, turning public opinion, particularly in the Islamic world, against America and deepening the divide between the West and Islamic world. In Pakistan, America's key ally in the campaign, the public opinion, which was earlier supportive of the President Musharraf's policy of unstinted co-operation with the United States, is turning increasingly hostile against this attack on a fellow Muslim nation.

General Musharraf is now caught in a cleft stick. At American pressure and arms-twisting he decided to make a policy of 'U' turn and ditch the Taliban and extend full support to America in its campaign against terror in Afghanistan. He justified this policy reversal as necessary in national interest. To the credit of General Musharraf, it must be said that he accepted the sudden and dramatic shift in the situation, understood that old pro-Taliban policy of the Pakistan Government lies buried in the debris of the World Trade Center and changed his stand accordingly. A less mentally supple leader would have fallen a martyr to his own rigidities. He also cleverly utilised the situation to consolidate his position. Earlier, under the cover of Agra summit, he quietly made himself the President. Now under the clouds of the Afghanistan war, he gave himself an open-ended extension as the Army Chief. He also reshuffled the Army Command. All the coup leaders, who stood by him two years ago, have now been either kicked upstairs or changed. General Mahmood, Corps Commander at Rawalpindi, who took over Islamabad and arrested Nawaz Shariff during October 1999 coup, and General Usmani, Corps Commander at Karachi, who took over the Karachi airport to ensure Musharraf's safe landing on his return from Colombo were relegated to unimportant posts, proving the maxim that power brooks neither rivals, nor a sense of obligation and an authoritarian ruler never likes to live under a shadow of gratitude. But the most startling change was the replacement of his old trusted friend, Mammod Ahmad, Chief of the Inter Services Intelligence (ISI), by Lt. General Eshan-ul-Haq, a moderate professional bereft of political ambitions. General Ahmad was a strong proponent of the pro-Taliban policies of the Pakistan Government and was opposed to this alliance with the U.S.A. He also supported Mullah Omar's adamant stand of not surrendering Osama. It is aptly said that in Pakistan's politics, the king-maker seldom outlasts the king. In 1971, Lt. Gen. Gul Hassan parted company with Yahya Khan and his coterie and played a key role in Zulfiqar Ali Bhutto's rise to power, but after appointing him as the Army Chief, Bhutto had been removed within 90 days.

The change of guard at the ISI was probably done at the promptings of the CIA, which complained of lack of co-operation from the ISI. India reportedly tipped off the USA that ISI financially backed the WTC suicide hijacker, Mohammad Atta. CIA's disenchantment with the ISI is bound to grow further in future. Indeed, it is very doubtful if the new ISI Chief will be able to control this "rogue elephant". The ISI has now become an invisible government with about 40 thousand officers and staff. It has thousands of Pashtun-speaking Pakistanis and freelance Afghan spies and has over the years developed very intimate contacts with the very heart of the terror network in Afghanistan. Though Musharraf has promised intelligence-sharing, it is very uncertain as to how much real help will be forthcoming from the ISI. Sometime during 1999, CIA's plot to train 60 Pakistani commandos to capture Bin Laden failed because at the last moment the ISI dragged its feet. Again, a very large number of ISI's officers as well as the field operatives embrace Islamic fundamentalism, and it is very unlikely that they would provide hard intelligence about Bin Laden, Mulla Omar and their cohorts. It will be very difficult, if not impossible, for the new ISI Chief to overhaul the agency filled with Islamic sympathisers. Further, the capacity of a powerful and well-entrenched intelligence apparatus to do mischief is immense and incalculable and there is great likelihood of the ISI clandestinely helping the Talibans and mounting covert operations in concert with the disaffected elements in the army to muddy the waters for Musharraf and put him on a tight spot.

In Pakistan, protests against Musharraf "policy of abjectly supporting the USA" are becoming louder and shriller. Initially, protests by the holy warriors and the agitated Afghan refugees, generally unemployed and unemployable (to use the words of the Pakistani journalist Irfan Hussain) were of manageable proportions and Musharraf placed their numbers at not more than 15 per cent of the population. Indeed, majority of the Pakistanis are moderates and not hard-headed jehadis. In fact, religious parties have never won five per cent of the national votes and sent more than six members to the national Assembly at any time. But these shock-troopers, who are getting increasingly armed, constitute a dangerous force because of their fervour and ferocity. And no Pakistani leader during the last twenty years has dared to stand upto them and call their bluff. The moderate public opinion in Pakistan, the silent majority, supported initially Musharraf's stand against the Islamic warriors. Thus, ironically in acknowledging and supporting moderate viewpoints, Musharraf, an unelected military ruler, has done what successive elected governments failed to achieve.

So far though cities, like Karachi, Quetta and Peshawar, have witnessed protest rallies, Punjab, the biggest province in Pakistan, has not boiled over, though the storm clouds are gathering. Incidentally, the Punjabis constitute 64 per cent of the Pakistan's army and 90 per cent of the officer cadre. But as the war drags on with unabated bombing, sometimes going off the targets and resulting in severe collateral damages, public mood in Pakistan is changing and becoming distinctly anti-American. This is compounding the worry of Musharraf, who wants quick and surgical action and speedy resolution of the Afghan crisis. If the Enduring Freedom endures for months, he will be trapped in a maze of problems.

Americans, however, have prepared themselves for a prolonged campaign. American strategies are aware that they are waging in Afghanistan a kind of combat unfamiliar to the Americans growing in the shadow of World War II, Korea, Vietnam and Persian Gulf. And this is a war in which the Americans have reconciled themselves to the risk of accepting casualties.

Even after three weeks of heavy bombing, the Talibans remain defiant and dug themselves in for a protracted guerrilla conflict by retreating to mountain redoubts, private homes and mosques to wait for the invading ground troops. Bin Laden and the Taliban are hoping to draw the U.S. into the trap that devoured the Soviet Union. As the war prolongs, the USA will expect more help from Pakistan and ask for not only logistical support, but secure bases from where they will be able to deploy their troops deep inside Afghanistan. This demand Musharraf will possibly find difficult to accommodate and the Pak-American relationship will gradually, but inevitably, turn sour.

At present, to mollify Pakistan and shore up its economic condition and boost the image of Musharraf, the West has promised economic assistance. A ban on military sales to Pakistan has been lifted and a new agreement eases the immediate burden of $ 329 million in debt on which Pakistan had defaulted. Washington has pledged $ 50 million in aid and Japan has come up with $ 41 million and European Union has matched that. India should not feel unhappy at this since a bankrupt Pakistan is not in India's national interest. Though economic assistance has started trickling in, it will be unrealistic to expect that all creditors will write off Pakistan's debts for which Musharraf is pressing. The Japanese have already indicated that they are reluctant to write off the debt, despite their support. Economic packages offered by Britain and United States fall short of wiping out Pakistan's $ 36 billion outstanding debt. Though Western assistance will enable Pakistan to avert immediate economic disaster, one Pakistani journalist (Ayaj Amir), has pointed out that $ 50 million gifted by Bush to Pakistan would be the cost of bombing Afghanistan for three or four days and the Americans have been able to get Pakistan's vital support at a cheap bargain.

It has to be borne in mind that Egypt's debt write off which is often quoted as a model for Pakistan's political and economic turnaround followed a fundamental change in Egypt's regional policy. Egypt recognised Israel and opted for a long-term regional settlement after signing the Camp David Accord. Before any debt write off, America will perhaps insist and ensure that Pakistan totally delinks itself from terrorism and makes a lasting peace with India under America sponsorship. Thus the USA, Japan and Western allies will bolster Pakistan in the short run and watch and wait for the future events to unfold themselves.

Another unintended impact of American bombing is that it has caused massive dislocation. Thousands of displaced Afghan refugees have become vulnerable to approaching

Afghan winter. This is likely to take a heavy toll of the lives of impoverished people of Afghanistan, who had nothing to do with the outrage of September 11. A human tragedy of gigantic proportions is round the corner. Because of the rising tide of anti-Americanism in Pakistan and sustained tirade against Musharraf by the radical Islamic parties, there is a distinct possibility of Musharraf being destabilised by the rabid elements in the Army acting in concert with the Islamic fundamentalists. Mullah-military nexus, which came into existence in the eighties remains quite strong and entrenched. This will create a terrible situation where the USA will have to think of plans to neutralise Pakistan's nuclear capabilities. Already, America has suggested to Pakistan to improve and strengthen the security of its nuclear assets as it is worried about nuclear weapons falling in wrong hands.

It is trying to persuade the Musharraf administration that a kind of joint command and control presence over Pakistan's nuclear programme is in their national interest. Arrest of Pakistan's nuclear experts on tip-off by the FBI for their links with the jehadi outfits must have aggravated USA's concern.

Again, though Pakistan is inveighing again North Alliance. America needs them for the messy ground operations. Already Collin Powel has made clear that the USA will not care much for Pakistan's view and feeling in this matter. It has been signed up for loyal service and paid the wages and should not protest too much.

Outcome of Afghan war remains unclear and uncertain. There is a real danger that it may trigger off chaos in Pakistan. A crisis unites countries. The opposite has happened in Pakistan. The current predicament has widened the cracks and divisions that may erode the cohesiveness of Pakistan. Unmanageable turmoil in Pakistan will not be in India's interest. We will be then at the receiving end of the detritus. Hence, developments in Pakistan have to be closely watched and counter-measures planned in advance.

Beleaguered rulers of Pakistan will definitely try to provoke troubles in Kashmir and other places in India as a diversionary move. *New York Times* has cautioned the U.S. against allowing Musharraf a free hand with regard to Islamic extremists in Kashmir. However, it is not known how far Washington at this stage will be able and willing to hold back Pakistan.

Induction of *Fidayen* (suicide squads) has introduced a new dimension in Kashmir militancy. The suicide squads may now try to strike against our vital assets not only in Kashmir, but in other places of the country. Military ripostes by India by crossing the LOC and attacking Pakistani terrorist centres is not practicable at the present juncture. This may boomerang on India and attract a large-scale war which will not be in her interest. However, a number of steps can be taken to improve our vigilance and enhance preparedness to foil sneak attacks by the terrorists. We have to plug holes in our security and intelligence apparatus. It is also necessary to educate the public of the terrorists, goals and tactics and ensure public support for the anti-terrorist measures by the government.

—1 November, 2001, The Statesman

13

Attack on Democracy : 13th December 2001, and After

Attack on Indian Parliament on December 13, 2001 is beyond doubt the most daring terrorist strike in the country during the last two decades. It was a vicious as well as an audacious attempt to wipe out, as Home Minister, L.K. Advani, said in his statement in the Parliament, the 'entire political leadership in a multi-party political system'. The incident has caused shock and indignation throughout the country and the overwhelming public mood is in favour of strong retaliatory action against the terrorists and their sponsors. They should not be allowed to get away unpunished is the popular cry. Investigation done so far has revealed that the suicidal attackers belonged to Jaish-e-Mohammad and Laskar-e-Toiba, two fanatical Jehadi outfits with headquarters in Pakistan, who are being supported and sustained by the ISI.

It is a matter of immense satisfaction that the audacious operations of terrorists could be effectively foiled by the police personnel guarding the Parliament. They displayed courage, efficiency and skill of a very high order and altogether nine of them died to save country's honour. Indeed, they do us proud. Though the suicide attackers were able to penetrate the peripheral control at the main gate, none of the five terrorists could enter the doors of the Lok Sabha building. It is learnt that the D.I.G. of Police in charge of the Parliament's Security Staff at the first noise of fire alerted his men at different gates and instructed them to close the gates. The security staff also because of the regular drill remained alert on their posts, unlike what had happened earlier during the attack on Srinagar Legislative Assembly. However, entry of the Ambassador car with a red flashing light on its roof and Home Ministry sticker through the main gate could not be prevented because there are almost more than one thousand of such cars going in and out of the Parliament. And cars in which the Members of the Parliament or their hangers-on move about are not properly checked or frisked mainly due to the non-cooperation of the M.Ps. It is unfortunate that no M.P., no V.I.P. or senior officer wants to be subjected to any security checks and the security staff performing the unpleasant duties are frowned on. The dignitaries also at times make exaggerated complaints.

The question that is now uppermost in every mind is how we respond to spiralling terrorist strikes. Regarding India's response, the Home Minister, whom the Pakistani Press describes as a 'super hawk', declared in the Parliament that the country was determined to stamp out terrorism. But rightly, he did not spell out any definite course of action. He, however, did not rule out any option. Indeed, in the face of this gravest provocation, India should carefully weigh all its options and work out its responses. Any thoughtless and adventurist action would serve the ends of the terrorists and their sponsors. Similarly, inaction would further encourage and embolden the terrorists to launch further attacks on other bastions of our democracy.

There is shrill demand from many quarters (including political leaders opposing tooth and nail any legislation to fight terrorism) to bomb the training camps of the terrorists in Pak occupied Kashmir. This is the constant refrain of the public statements emanating from different groups and parties. But the fact to be remembered is that at present, there are no visible training camps in Pakistan. These camps are no more than 'drill squares and firing ranges'. Further, military and security experts are also of the clear view that though the Indian Army has an edge over the Pakistani Army in respect of numerical strength and conventional weapons, the military balance is not preponderantly in our favour. Hot pursuit or surgical air-strikes will bring in their wake retaliatory attacks and may escalate into an all-out war. India is in no position to emulate the U.S.A. or Israel in launching massive air-strikes against the terrorists or their mentors. Again, Pakistan is no push-over. In a conventional all-out war, India has definite advantages, but Pakistan may nuclearise the conflict. Pakistan's low threshold of nuclear tolerance is a worry, of course, any nuclear war will devastate India, but will be catastrophic for Pakistan. It will sign its death-warrant. However, it is difficult to be sure if the rabid elements in Pakistani Army would act within a framework that others would call rational.

Both the U.S.A. and Russia have called for restraint, the familiar appeal in any Indo-Pakistan crisis. Collin Powel, U.S. Secretary of State, had for the first time recognised that India has a 'legitimate right of self-defence', but counselled against military retaliation. Powel said that U.S. would like India to remember that there was a law of unintended consequences and none wanted a limited military retaliation to turn to a full-fledged war. Further, United States, in a clear reference to militant organisations that have links to Kashmir movement, has asked Islamabad to take action against 'terrorist groups that operate out of Pakistan'. It is clear that at the present stage of the Afghan conflict, U.S.A. is not going to withdraw support for Musharraf. The White House spokesman, Ari Fleircher, has appreciated "superb" co-operation from Pakistan to fight the war against terrorism in Afghanistan. The U.S.A. wants to hold the attack on Parliament as an independent operation by Pakistan-based terrorists. It is possible that Pakistan government may not be directly involved in this terrorist strike on Parliament, but it is unlikely to rein in the jehadi outfits.

So India has to work out its own strategy to fight the war against terrorism. A number of carefully calculated proactive steps can be initiated to firmly deal with cross-border terrorism, and particularly the dangers posed by the suicidal terrorists.

First, diplomatic activities have to be stepped up to ensure that full pressure of the international community is brought on Pakistan to end cross-border terrorism. India must embark on a diplomatic offensive and garner the support of the international community. Second, after thorough and painstaking investigation, India should prepare a water-tight case regarding the involvement of the Pakistan-based terrorist outfits in this attack on Parliament and make the results of our investigation available to the FBI. Pakistan will always try to punch holes in the evidence gathered by Indian investigative agencies. It has criticised Indian 'duplicity' in rejecting American suggestion of involving the FBI with the investigation. But if Indian investigation bears the stamp of FBI approval, Musharraf may be forced by the U.S. and international pressure to go for a crackdown on the jehadis. The latest statement of President Bush that other states must help India tackle terrorism is an indicator of American thinking in this matter. Third, India must withdraw all one-sided privileges granted to Pakistan including most favoured nation treatment. Fourth, to make the proxy war costly and hurtful to Pakistan, India should not hesitate to launch a counter proxy war. At present, military establishment in Pakistan is carrying on the proxy war at little cost to itself and will continue to do so unless we make the cost prohibitive to Pakistan. Till now, India has considered economic and political price of containing insurgency in Kashmir manageable. But the restraint cannot endure indefinitely. India has now perhaps to think in terms of covert, deniable and determined operations that will hurt Pakistan politically as well as economically. After Afghan conflict, Pakistan is now a veritable tinder-box and it is possible to unleash the dogs of sectarian strife and ethnic tension in Baluchistan and North Western Frontier Province. So long, it was conventional wisdom that stable and united Pakistan was in India's security interests. But in view of Pakistan's persistent belligerence, a fragmented Pakistan would perhaps pose lesser problems than the united country. It will be India's riposte to Pakistan's game of dismembering India by 'thousand cuts'.

Fifth, we have to plug the loopholes in our security and intelligence apparatus. It is true that induction of *fidayeen* has introduced a new dimension to security threats in Kashmir and elsewhere in the country. But security forces are not exactly helpless in the face of *fidayeen* attacks. Constant vigilance and preparedness can and has foiled many of these attacks. Sixth, in all important government buildings and installations, our V.I.Ps. and senior officers must not only unfailingly submit themselves to security checks and drill that may at time cause inconvenience to them but also encourage and co-operate with the security staff doing onerous but unpleasant duties. Similarly, professionalism and perceptiveness of the security staff must also improve.

—4th January 2002, The Statesman

14

More Terrorist Strikes are in the Offing

Terrorist car bomb strikes near U.S. Consulate in Karachi are ominous portents of more sinister developments in the coming days. Under intense international pressure Musharraf promised to choke off infiltration of the militants into Kashmir and the U.S. Secretary of State, Collin Powel, expressed the hope that the flow of infiltrators was going to stop permanently. Many in India have viewed this as a triumph of India's coercive diplomacy. However, any such euphoric assessment will be premature and misplaced. There is every likelihood that Musharraf may keep quiet for some time and then again quietly and unobtrusively allow the infiltration of militants into Kashmir. However, it will now be difficult for him to sponsor terrorism under the gaze of the international community. Addressing the House of Commons, the British Foreign Secretary, Jack Straw, has now unambiguously said that there is a direct link between the ISI and some of the hardcore terrorist groups in Pakistan. Musharraf will have to tread warily.

Pakistan's military rulers thought that by joining the U.S. coalition against terror, they would be able to protect their proxy war in Kashmir. Addressing the people of Pakistan last September, Musharraf said that "he was joining the lesser evil (America) to fight the greater evil (India)". He has also serious domestic compulsions. Kashmir is a very emotive issue in Pakistan. Pakistan's army and the I.S.I. are totally involved in training and sending the jehadis to Kashmir to fight holy war for the last eleven years and Musharraf himself has been one of the foremost champions of this policy of 'breaking India by thousand cuts'. International community now wants Musharraf to take an immediate unilateral about-turn on Kashmir as he did in the case of Afghanistan. This poses an acute dilemma for him and also for the Pakistani army and Pakistan nation. Quest for '*Kashmir banega Pakistan*' cannot be given up so easily. Abandonment of this policy will be viewed by the public in Pakistan as a sell-out to India under American pressure.

Further, Musharraf's position has weakened after the spurious referendum. It has also eroded the credibility of his regime as nearly 90 per cent of the people supported the opposition parties' call for a boycott and did not go to the polling booths. Reports indicate that some of the Corps Commanders also opposed April 30 referendum. Though Pakistan's army, by and large, has remained loyal to the General, there are elements inside the army and the I.S.I. sympathetic to the *jehadis* and their support and sympathy for the militants will become more pronounced as Musharraf's authority weakens.

Again, India plans to hold free and fair election in Kashmir in autumn and is trying to persuade the moderate separatists to participate. Pakistan fears that if the turn-out in the election is high, and if the new government appears to be popular, then it will strengthen India's stand that the Kashmiris have decided their future.

The fluid situation is compounded by another ominous development. Many Al-Qaida fighters from Afghanistan have now shifted into Pakistan and are trying to regroup in the tribal regions of Pakistan. So far only two out of twenty two Al-Qaida leaders could be arrested. The U.S. intelligence believes that Bin Laden along with his deputy Aiyman-al-Zawahir, the Dick Cheney of Al-Qaida (as *Time Magazine* has called him), is hiding in mountains along Pakistan-Afghanistan border and is still capable of getting messages out to his followers. Operations of the elite British and American commandos to track them down have not so far been successful. American bombings thus have dispersed and not eliminated the terrorists.

Francis Taylor, the U.S. State Department's counter-terrorism co-ordinator, believes that Al-Qaida is going to launch serious terrorist attacks soon. And the main targets will be the U.S.A. and India, and the latter will be an easier and more vulnerable target. Some Al-Qaida cells are sleepers, remaining inactive for long periods while others will launch attack without waiting for a green signal from a central authority. Abu Zubaydah, Al-Qaida's Chief of Operations, who was captured in Faislabad, Pakistan, has provided many valuable leads to the U.S. interrogators which helped the detection of three Saudi Al-Qaida members planning an attack on NATO warship in the Strait of Gibraltar. The U.S. Attorney General, John Ashcoft, announced the capture in Chicago of Jose Padille, an American citizen calling himself Abdullah-al-Muhazir. Padille was working out a plan to build and detonate a radiological dispersal device.

There is also another point to be borne in mind. India also must acknowledge the hard fact that even the most committed government in Islamabad will not be able to eliminate terrorism totally from Kashmir. There are many terrorist groups inside and outside Pakistan, who are against Musharraf for ditching the Talibans and now working overtime to settle score with him. Terrorist groups function as loose cells and their operations are not always being guided or co-ordinated by any central agency. There is no doubt that Musharraf should do more to prevent cross-border terrorism, but he is no longer in full control of events in Pakistan. Only demonising Musharraf will preclude any rational engagement with Pakistan. India should try to provide some cover to Musharraf to show that he is not selling out a defining national cause.

America's sub-continental agenda is to enhance the capabilities of both India and Pakistan in fighting against the challenge of terrorism. It does not want to do anything at this stage of the war against Al-Qaida to destabilise Musharraf and opt for an unknown successor. During his testimony before the Senate Committee last March, CIA Director Tenet said that the decision to turn Islamabad into an ally in the wake of terrorist strikes on September 11 was a 'fundamental political shift with inherent risks'.

Meanwhile, we must gird up our loins and brace ourselves against serious terrorist strikes in Kashmir and other parts of the country. The security forces in Jammu and Kashmir are gradually getting better of the terrorists and the kill ratio in the counter-terrorist operations is now 12:1 in favour of the Indian Army. Hence, spectacular kamikaze strikes by terrorist outfits who want to draw international attention and also queer the pitch for Musharraf are likely. To deal with the likely eventuality, we have to plug the loopholes in our security and intelligence apparatus. It is difficult to get pinpointed and predictive intelligence about terrorist operations, but constant preparedness and vigilance can foil many of their attacks. It is also seen that information available about terrorist strikes is not sometimes properly analysed, evaluated and disseminated. FBI agent Rowley's bomb shell letter now indicts the FBI for downplaying and glossing over the reports on the terrorist operations mounted on September 11. A series of target-hardening measures are called for. It is further necessary to educate the public of terrorist goals and tactics and ensure public support for various anti-terrorist measures adopted by the government.

—26 June, 2002, The Statesman

15

Suicide Bombers

Suicide attacks are increasingly becoming standard techniques of violence of a large number of terrorist outfits. Suicide terrorism first hogged the limelight when in April, 1983, the terrorist network of Hizbullah attacked the American Embassy in Beirut and later the same year devastated the U.S. Marine Headquarters in Lebanon. Hizbullah's successful strikes inspired the Liberation Tigers of Tamil Elam (LTTE) to resort to suicide bombings in a big way in their terror campaigns in Sri Lanka.

On July 5, 1987, Captain Miller of LTTE drove an explosive-laden truck into a Sri Lanka army camp in Northern Jaffna peninsula killing more than 1000 soldiers. Since then LTTE cadres have carried out more than 150 suicide attacks and about 243 Tigers including 53 women have taken part in them. The suicide bombers are known as "Black Tigers" and July 5 is celebrated by LTTE as a day of "Black Tigers" when a number of ceremonies are performed and the families of suicide bombers are honoured. The Black Tiger is separated from ordinary cadres and severs all contact with family and friends.

Lethal mission

Black Tigers are the only group, which succeeded in assassinating two former Prime Ministers — Rajiv Gandhi and Premadasa. Before embarking on suicide mission, the

Black Tigers would partake in a special meal with LTTE Supremo, V. Prabhakaran. According to Prabhakaran (quoted in a Tamil daily): "The suicide squad came into being at a critical juncture of the liberation movement and have taken it to the next stage."

It is very difficult to detect the suicide bombers. Their operations are very carefully planned and details meticulously worked out. Babu, the LTTE Cadre who killed Premadasa, infiltrated into his staff and remained inactive for about two years before carrying out his lethal mission.

In their struggle against Israel, Palestinian militants groups are increasingly resorting to suicide attacks against Israeli targets and this has become an effective and very potent weapon in the hands of the Palestinian militant groups. Most of the bombers are affiliated to terrorist outfits like Hamas or Islamic *Jihad*. The majority of the Palestinian suicide bombers are unmarried young men in their late teens who are recruited from mosques, schools and religious institutions. Recruits are reassured before assassination that their families will be looked after their martyrdom and there are charitable organisations that exist for this purpose. The explosives they carry have a hand-operated detonator rather than a button to minimise chances of accidental explosion. Although not exactly crude, the personal bombs are cheap.

According to some Israeli experts the total material for each cost about $ 150. Suicide bombing is thus an incredibly cost-effective method of terrorism, especially when the perpetrators do not care for their lives. Experts who have studied the background of the suicide bombers in the Middle East have found that they tended to have fanatical and authoritarian personality and many of them come from orthodox "marginal Muslim background". The recruiters from Hamas look for two qualities in a potential bomber: an intense interest in Islam and a clean criminal record so as not to raise the suspicion of Israel's Secret Service.

New Front

However, in Chechnya many of the suicide bombers are wives and relatives of rebels who want to avenge their loved ones killed in Chechnya's decade-long war with Russia. Very often their reasons are personal rather than religious or political. Very recently suicide bombings by Chechen terrorists killed more than forty people in a packed commuter train in Russia.

In Iraq suicide bombers have now opened a new front and kept American occupying forces on tenterhooks. In an unequal fight in terms of weaponry and resources suicide bombing has become a very potent weapon of resistance. The fact that no names and records of the suicide bombers are available in several instances point to the suspected involvement of foreign Islamic organisations.

Recent twin suicide bombings in Istanbul in Turkey, which took the lives of 32 people, most of them Turkish citizens, and wounded more than 450 carried the stamp of Al-Qaida's operational style of using suicide bombers to launch multiple attacks at soft targets. Though there is no evidence that Al-Qaida has regrouped itself as a force to reckon with, it has indeed become a mentor for the local terrorist groups who provide the cannon fodders — the suicide bombers.

The ultimate suicide terrorists revealed themselves on 11 September, 2001 by slamming commercial jets in the World Trade Centre. But the terrorists who participated in the attacks generally came from comfortable backgrounds and were older and better educated than the typical suicide bombers.

In the Indian context suicide terrorism was not known in the early years of terrorism in Punjab and Jammu and Kashmir. In India first manifestation of the suicide strike was assassination of Rajiv Gandhi in 1991 and the killing of Punjab chief minister Beant Singh in Chandigarh in August,

1995. In Jammu and Kashmir indigenous terrorist groups seldom involve themselves in acts of suicide bombing and such strikes have been the handiworks of trained and motivated foreign mercenaries. However, the Fidayeen attacks in which ISI-backed outfits like Jaish-I-Muhammad, Laskar-i-Toiba, Hizbul Mujahideen are involved have changed the security scenario. The terrorists are carrying out their strikes in a daring and very effective way. They are openly taking on security forces, at locations otherwise considered secure and engaging themselves in many protracted and determined encounters.

Unique Situation

As a result, among security forces casualties have sharply increased in the last two years. About 80 security personnel have lost their lives in 50 Fidayeen attacks. Kashmir is a unique situation in which suicide missions are executed by those not belonging to Kashmir but fighting for Kashmiri cause. Suicide attacks in Kashmir are mostly religious in nature and not national.

It is extremely difficult to prevent suicide attacks by committed groups who are in a position always to spring a surprise. Nevertheless, measures can be devised to minimise the impact of such attacks by making the task of suicide bombers more difficult through the strengthening of physical security measures, strict access control and tightening of verification procedures. There is also need for upgradation of awareness and alertness among the security force personnel deployed for protection of sensitive installations and other vulnerable targets. Regular briefing of security personnel and testing of their response to different situations through simulated exercise is necessary. Along with this, there should be upgradation of equipments and weaponry available to security personnel guarding vulnerable premises and personalities.

While analyzing the motivations of the suicide bombers

it is also necessary to bear in mind that people who carry out suicide bombings that deliberately target the civilians are guilty of crimes against humanity. They are not martyrs but war criminals. The scale and systemic nature of these attacks set them apart from other attacks committed in times of conflict. They are guilty of crime against humanity and should be brought to justice.

—24 December, 2003, Statesman

Index